New Directions for Community Colleges

Arthur M. Cohen
EDITOR-IN-CHIEF

Richard L. Wagoner
ASSOCIATE EDITOR

Gabriel Jones
MANAGING EDITOR

Institutional Effectiveness

Ronald B. Head
EDITOR

Number 153 • Spring 2011
Jossey-Bass
San Francisco

INSTITUTIONAL EFFECTIVENESS
Ronald B. Head (ed.)
New Directions for Community Colleges, no. 153

Arthur M. Cohen, Editor-in-Chief
Richard L. Wagoner, Associate Editor
Gabriel Jones, Managing Editor

NEW DIRECTIONS FOR COMMUNITY COLLEGES (ISSN 0194-3081, electronic ISSN 1536-0733) is part of The Jossey-Bass Higher and Adult Education Series and is published quarterly by Wiley Subscription Services, Inc., A Wiley Company, at Jossey-Bass, 989 Market Street, San Francisco, CA 94103-1741. Periodicals Postage Paid at San Francisco, California, and at additional mailing offices. POSTMASTER: Send address changes to New Directions for Community Colleges, Jossey-Bass, 989 Market Street, San Francisco, CA 94103-1741.

SUBSCRIPTIONS cost $89.00 for individuals and $259.00 for institutions, agencies, and libraries in the United States. Prices subject to change.

EDITORIAL CORRESPONDENCE should be sent to the Editor-in-Chief, Arthur M. Cohen, at the Graduate School of Education and Information Studies, University of California, Box 951521, Los Angeles, CA 90095-1521. All manuscripts receive anonymous reviews by external referees.

New Directions for Community Colleges is indexed in CIJE: Current Index to Journals in Education (ERIC), Contents Pages in Education (T&F), Current Abstracts (EBSCO), Ed/Net (Simpson Communications), Education Index/Abstracts (H. W. Wilson), Educational Research Abstracts Online (T&F), ERIC Database (Education Resources Information Center), and Resources in Education (ERIC).

Microfilm copies of issues and articles are available in 16mm and 35mm, as well as microfiche in 105mm, through University Microfilms Inc., 300 North Zeeb Road, Ann Arbor, MI 48106-1346.

Contents

EDITOR'S NOTES

Institutional effectiveness lies at the heart of both accreditation and accountability as regional accrediting all agencies, state legislatures, and even the federal government increasingly ask all colleges to demonstrate their effectiveness in all aspects of their operation. As Ewell noted in 2001, most higher education institutions "require institutions or programs to examine student achievement or 'institutional effectiveness' as part of their self-study and review processes" (p. 3). Indeed, in recent years, all six regional accrediting agencies have developed and strengthened institutional effectiveness requirements, mandating in effect that institutional effectiveness be fully measured and reported at nearly every community college in the country. In 2006, the federal government became involved as the Secretary of Education's Commission on the Future recommended that information on cost, price, student achievement, and student success be "reported publicly in aggregate form to provide consumers and policymakers an accessible, understandable way to measure the relative effectiveness of different colleges and universities" (p. 4).

Given the attention that both external agencies and community colleges are paying to institutional effectiveness, it is somewhat surprising that so few books and articles on the subject appear in the literature. A recent search of the ERIC database using the term *institutional effectiveness* revealed 647 results; limiting the search to sources containing the term *community colleges*, as well as *institutional effectiveness*, yielded 317 results. A search using the term *assessment* revealed 100,564 results, and limiting the search to sources containing community colleges yielded 5,415 results. This lack of coverage is both unfortunate and somewhat perplexing, as institutional effectiveness is a concept that encompasses assessment and includes much more. What seems to have happened is that the term *institutional effectiveness* has become so commonly accepted that few consider it as separate from its components. In this respect, institutional effectiveness is a whole that includes such pieces as assessment and evaluation, but it is the pieces that are typically written about and not the whole. A (w)holistic approach to institutional effectiveness, coalescing all of the pieces into a seamless whole, which is the intent of this volume, should prove invaluable to community college scholars and practitioners alike and be a significant contribution to the literature.

In Chapter One, I trace the origins of institutional effectiveness in higher education, describe its evolution, and present a brief history of the use of the term *institutional effectiveness* by colleges, universities, community colleges, accrediting agencies, and statewide systems of higher education. The chapter culminates with a practical, operational definition of *institutional effectiveness*. In Chapter Two, Terri Manning describes the overall organizational process of institutional effectiveness as practiced in American community colleges, as well as individual processes and practices typically included in a comprehensive model. A major focus of the chapter is the cyclical nature of institutional effectiveness.

Chapter Three explores the relationship between institutional effectiveness and the accountability movement in higher education. Peter Ewell discusses external pressures on community colleges by accrediting agencies, the federal government, state governments, and the general public to provide more meaningful information on student learning, student learning outcomes, and other accountability measures. In addition, Ewell reflects on how accountability will evolve and affect community colleges in the coming years. The focus shifts from accountability to accreditation in Chapter Four. Michael Johnson and I explore the influence of accreditation on institutional effectiveness in community colleges, briefly mentioning institutional effectiveness requirements in each of the six regional accrediting agencies and providing a case study within the SACSCOC region showing that accreditation standards viewed as best practices can provide numerous benefits to community colleges.

Chapter Five not only touches on accreditation but also on how institutional effectiveness has affected, and been affected by, the more traditional concept of institutional research. George Johnston uses case studies to explore how different community college offices of institutional research are organized and how they function in the process of measuring institutional effectiveness and responding to accreditation requirements. The purpose of Chapter Six is to identify key ways in which academic program review provides information and documentation demonstrating that a community college is effective. Trudy Bers discusses both the positive outcomes of program review and its challenges and presents different models of program review.

Student success, the focus of Chapter Seven, is at the heart of both institutional effectiveness and the community college mission, yet measuring such success at community colleges is problematic. Chris Baldwin, Estela Bensimon, Alicia Dowd, and Lisa Kleiman present commonly used measures of student success, analyze their strengths and weaknesses, and discuss innovative measures being used in benchmark community colleges throughout the United States. In Chapter Eight, Willard Hom discusses the impact that various stakeholders have on the practice of institutional effectiveness in community colleges. He notes differences in perceptions among these stakeholders and provides a framework for understanding their concerns and issues.

The concluding chapter speculates about the future of institutional effectiveness in American community colleges. Richard Alfred offers recommendations and suggestions about how institutional effectiveness will evolve, as well as how it can be improved today in community colleges.

Ronald B. Head
Editor

References

Ewell, P. *Accreditation and Student Learning Outcomes: A Proposed Point of Departure.* Washington, D.C.: Council for Higher Education Accreditation, 2001.
Secretary of Education's Commission on the Future. *A Test of Leadership: Charting the Future of U.S. Higher Education.* Washington, D.C.: U.S. Department of Education, 2006.

RONALD B. HEAD *serves as a special projects officer at Tidewater Community College in Norfolk, Virginia; teaches doctoral education courses online for the University of Phoenix; and does consulting work in accreditation and institutional effectiveness.*

1

The origins of institutional effectiveness are traced, its evolution within community colleges is described, the use of the term institutional effectiveness *is analyzed, and a practical, operational definition of the term is presented.*

The Evolution of Institutional Effectiveness in the Community College

Ronald B. Head

Although it is uncertain when the term *institutional effectiveness* was first used—at least in the context of higher education—or who coined it, it first gained attention in December 1984 when the Commission on Colleges (COC) of the Southern Association of Colleges and Schools (SACS) adopted it in its revision of institutional accreditation requirements. The executive director of the commission at that time, James Rogers (1997), recalled that *institutional effectiveness* was chosen because *assessment* was too contentious a term. "So controversial and even intimidating was the 'A word' that new terminology had to be found to give a broader and more acceptable definition to the concept," Rogers wrote. "That new term was *institutional effectiveness*" (p. 1).

Two decades later, Goben (2007) noted, "Institutional Effectiveness has become so important to colleges and universities that the language is embedded in accreditation and strategic efforts" (p. 1). Still, despite its undisputed importance and widespread use, *institutional effectiveness* is a term commonly used but seldom defined. Community college educators use it frequently, almost glibly, but seldom pause to consider any differences between it and similar terms such as *assessment* or *evaluation*.

Assessment was a contentious topic in 1984, because a year earlier, the influential report *A Nation at Risk* (National Commission on Excellence in Education, 1983) had ignited already simmering debates concerning the public accountability of educational institutions. Although nowhere in the report

NEW DIRECTIONS FOR COMMUNITY COLLEGES, no. 153, Spring 2011 © 2011 Wiley Periodicals, Inc.
Published online in Wiley Online Library (wileyonlinelibrary.com) • DOI: 10.1002/cc.432

did the word *accountability* appear and the focus of the report was not on higher education but on the K-12 sector of education, colleges and universities were not immune from the pressures directed to elementary, middle, and high schools. In fact, nearly a decade earlier, Folger (1977) predicted that the public would increasingly demand more accountability from colleges—something that certainly came about—and noted that while in the past, financial accountability was all that was required, "accountability for results and effective performance [was] now expected" (p. 91). In other words, Folger was referring to the burgeoning concept of institutional effectiveness.

Folger also wrote that performance measures in higher education "create special problems because of the historic autonomy of colleges and universities regarding their academic programs and functions" and that "there [was] little agreement about how much of any assessment or review can be left to the institution itself and how much should be undertaken by other state agencies—and by which agencies, at that" (p. 91). He concluded by warning that "if higher education leaders do not help answer questions about desirable assessment process and standards, answers will be supplied by others" (p. 94)—a warning that in many states went unheeded and, as we now know, led state agencies to assume greater control of academic program review and student assessment, often to the detriment or dismay of colleges and universities.

The Three A's of Institutional Effectiveness

To understand not only the origins of institutional effectiveness but also the concept itself, we need to examine it in the context of what I refer to as the three A's: assessment, accreditation, and accountability (Head, 2008b).

Assessment, usually used in the context of student learning and learning outcomes, is an integral part of institutional effectiveness. Indeed, as Rogers noted, when SACS adopted the concept of institutional effectiveness, it was synonymous with assessment (though it has since evolved considerably beyond this). Muffo (2001) noted that "a basic definition of assessment would take into account the fundamental shift on inputs to one on outcomes." He explains that "using such factors as college rankings, funding, faculty degrees, and library holdings are input-driven," while considering "the end product of education, or what students learn," is outcomes-driven. Interestingly, while Muffo wrote that "the first question to be addressed regarding assessment has to do with its definition" (p. 60), he in fact never defined the term.

The significance that *accreditation* has had on institutional effectiveness can be seen by the very fact that SACS was largely responsible for introducing the concept to institutions of higher education. Accrediting agencies started proposing moving from inputs to outputs as early as the late 1970s, and today all six regional agencies strongly advocate the importance of institutional effectiveness. As Dodd (2004) wrote, "Accreditation constitutes an important motivation to initiate outcomes assessment efforts" (p. 15). Indeed, the fact that accreditors require community colleges to demonstrate compliance with institutional effectiveness standards ensures that every community college in the United States emphasizes institutional effectiveness. In essence, then, accreditation guarantees that institutional effectiveness is a concept that will never fade away.

Accountability, the third "A" in my triumvirate, stemmed from funding and enrollment declines in the 1970s that affected the quality of American higher education. Accountability was largely driven by external forces, as all levels of government, accrediting agencies, students, and the public increasingly demanded that colleges and universities be held responsible for their product. Pressures to demonstrate institutional effectiveness arose—and continue to arise—as a result of such factors as the cost of higher education, the inability of college graduates to find meaningful employment, employer dissatisfaction with graduates' skills and knowledge, accrediting agency requirements, attacks on academe from those within higher education, news stories criticizing colleges and universities, and the glacial nature of change within higher education (Head, 2008b).

From a different perspective, as Rossman and El-Khawas (1987) note, the institutional effectiveness movement has been driven by three primary forces: political, economic, and educational. Political pressures have come about from perceived weaknesses in higher education and the public's demand to know whether the high cost of higher education is justified. From an economic viewpoint, institutional effectiveness is a way of ensuring that the workforce to support national, state, and local economies is well trained and competent. Finally, as we have seen, such educational reports as *A Nation at Risk* (National Commission on Excellence in Education, 1983) have called for assessing institutional quality. Erwin (1991) proposed a fourth force: societal, or the need for society to understand how higher education meets public needs.

Institutional Effectiveness and the Criteria for Accreditation

Because the term *institutional effectiveness* came into the vocabulary of higher education as a result of SACS, it might prove helpful to see how SACS has used the term. The *Criteria for Accreditation* were approved by the COC in December 1984. At the time, one institutional researcher quipped that the criteria were a guaranteed meal ticket for institutional researchers. According to section 3 of the *Criteria* (1998), "The concept of institutional effectiveness is at the heart of the Commission's philosophy of accreditation and is central to instructional programs and operations. It pervades the *Criteria for Accreditation*" (p. 17). The preamble goes on to state, "Although evaluation of educational quality and effectiveness is a difficult task requiring careful analysis and professional judgment, each member institution is expected to document quality and effectiveness by employing a comprehensive system of planning and evaluation in all major aspects of the institution" (p. 17).

The institutional effectiveness criteria were never prescriptive, which is perhaps one reason that the term is used so imprecisely. The preamble to the *Criteria* states:

> The Commission advocates no single interpretation of the concept of institutional effectiveness. It does, however, expect each member institution to develop a broad-based system to determine institutional effectiveness appropriate to its own context and purpose, to use the purpose statement as the foundation for planning and evaluation, to employ a variety of assessment methods, and to demonstrate use of the results of the planning and evaluation process for the improvement of both educational programs and support activities [Commission on Colleges, 1998, p. 17].

Interestingly, nowhere in the *Criteria for Accreditation* was the term *institutional effectiveness* defined, though in 2005, on page 9 of the SACS *Resource Manual for the Principles of Accreditation*, *institutional effectiveness* is defined as "the systematic, explicit, and documented process of measuring performance against mission in all aspects of an institution" (Commission on Colleges, 2005, p. 9). This is a good, though broad, definition, especially in relation to accreditation, but it came two decades after SACS adopted the concept.

The Institutional Effectiveness Cycle

Based on the SACS *Criteria*, institutional effectiveness evolved into a cyclical process linking institutional purpose with institutional improvement. To conceptualize this process, I have had students of institutional effectiveness think in terms of a circle (Head, 2008c; see also Brandt, 1998, p. 5). As Figure 1.1 shows, the top is Purpose, which points down toward the right toward Goals or Objectives, and then to the bottom, toward Evaluation, then back up to the left toward Use of Results, and then, finally, completing

Figure 1.1. The Cyclical Nature of Institutional Effectiveness

the circle, back up to the top, toward Purpose. The purpose of a community college—its programs and services as written in a mission statement—drives the institutional effectiveness process, because what community colleges want to do is show whether and how well that purpose is fulfilled. From the purpose, the college formulates goals or objectives, which are similar to directions on a map, used to determine whether the purpose is achieved. Evaluation, which in this case is synonymous with *assessment*, is the process of measuring the goals and objectives to determine whether they were accomplished and whether they met certain expectations, or standards. Using these evaluation results, community colleges can determine whether the purpose is appropriate, refine it as necessary, and in the process improve their programs and services.

Most community college practitioners assume they understand the concept of institutional effectiveness without worrying about its definition. Yet as David S. Webster noted, institutional effectiveness "means different things to different people" (cited by Malone, 2003, p. 31). Indeed, a cursory examination of the literature and relevant Web sites reveals only a handful of definitions prior to 2005. The following is comprehensive but perhaps too cumbersome to gain widespread appeal:

> Institutional Effectiveness . . . is the condition of achieving the set goals of an institution and being able to verify the attainment of these goals with specific data which show the degree or quality of their attainment. Where the principal goal or goals of the institution relate to instruction and student services, emphasis is placed on student outcomes assessment. Institutional effectiveness data include measures of *effectiveness, productivity, efficiency,* and relative *excellence or quality* [McLeod and Atwell, 1992, p. 34].

Institutional Effectiveness Defined

Rogers' assertion that the term *institutional effectiveness* was used in the *Criteria for Accreditation* because *assessment* was too contentious a word might lead to the assumption that the two terms are synonymous. As we have already seen, Muffo (2001) addressed the relationship of assessment to institutional effectiveness but never defined either term. Bauer (2001) discussed definitions of *assessment*, noting that "many higher education officials hold different interpretations of assessment" (p. 9). She presented a number of different definitions from the literature, ranging from ones narrowly focused on student learning to broader ones encompassing entire systems of higher education. To the extent that both *assessment* and *institutional effectiveness* are broadly and often contradictorily defined, they are synonymous. Yet other terms, such as *evaluation, quality review,* and even *efficiency,* are used synonymously with *assessment* and *institutional effectiveness*. In fact, *institutional research* is often used interchangeably with *institutional effectiveness*. The question, then, is how to distinguish among these various terms.

Figure 1.2. The Components of Institutional Effectiveness

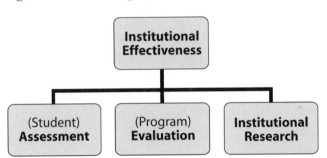

One answer is to consider *institutional effectiveness* as an umbrella term covering related terms such as *evaluation, institutional research, assessment,* or *outcomes analysis*. In this sense, as Figure 1.2 shows, we can envision *institutional effectiveness* as a broader term encompassing assessment (in terms of student assessment), evaluation (in terms of program evaluation), and institutional research. Institutional effectiveness is a broad-scaled, institution-wide process consisting of specific components, including the evaluation of all academic programs, administrative units, and support services; the assessment of student learning outcomes; and data-driven support by the institutional research arm of a college or university (Head, 2008a).

This approach simply but effectively defines *institutional effectiveness*. Drawing on the definitions of the two words making up the term, *institutional* and *effectiveness*, we can construct a rough but utilitarian definition. *Institutional* refers to the community college as a whole, so *institutional effectiveness* applies to every aspect of the community college. *Effectiveness* refers to quality, so institutional effectiveness measures the quality of the community college. In this sense, "Institutional effectiveness is the process and structure used by a college to determine the quality of its students, academic programs, administrative functions, and support services" (Head, 2008a, p. 8).

I hope that this definition and the discussion in this chapter prove useful to community college administrators, instructors, and scholars interested in community colleges. Ultimately institutional effectiveness is important not only because it permeates all aspects of a community college, but because it strips away the confounding rhetoric too often found on community college campuses to illuminate why the college exists (its purpose) and what it does well (its quality). How it does this—or the process used by community colleges—is the focus of Chapter Two.

References

Bauer, K. "Assessment for Institutional Research: Guidelines and Resources." In W. E. Knight (ed.), *The Primer for Institutional Research*. Tallahassee, Fla.: Association for Institutional Research, 2001.

Brandt, D. M. "Institutional Effectiveness: Practice or Theory." Paper presented at the 38th Annual Forum of the Association of Institutional Research, Minneapolis, Minn., May 17–20, 1998.

Commission on Colleges. *Criteria for Accreditation.* (12th ed.) Atlanta, Ga.: Southern Association of Colleges and Schools, 1998.

Commission on Colleges. *Resource Manual for the Principles of Accreditation: Foundations for Quality Enhancement.* Decatur, Ga.: Southern Association of Colleges and Schools, 2005. http://www.sacscoc.org/pdf/handbooks/Exhibit%2031.Resource%20Manual.pdf.

Dodd, A. H. "Accreditation as a Catalyst for Institutional Effectiveness." Successful Strategic Planning: New Directions for Institutional Research, no. 123, eds. Michael Dooris, John Kelley, James F. Trainer. San Francisco: Jossey-Bass, 2004.

Erwin, T. D. *Assessing Student Learning and Development: A Guide to the Principles, Goals, and Methods of Determining College Outcomes.* San Francisco: Jossey-Bass, 1991.

Folger, J. K. (ed.). "Increasing the Public Accountability of Higher Education." New Directions for Institutional Research, no. 16, ed. John K. Folger. San Francisco: Jossey-Bass, 1977.

Goben, A. (2007). "FanSAStic! Results: Collaboratively Leading Institutional Effectiveness Efforts in Higher Education Institutions." Paper presented at the SAS Global Forum, Las Vegas, NV, 2007.

Head, R. B. "Defining Institutional Effectiveness." C2IR LearnNet, IE 101, "Institutional Effectiveness," Topic 1, Lesson 2. Gainesville: University of Florida, 2008a.

Head, R. B. "Historical Overview Institutional Effectiveness." C2IR LearnNet, IE 101 "Institutional Effectiveness," Topic 1, Lesson 1. Gainesville: University of Florida, 2008b.

Head, R. B. "The Institutional Effectiveness Process." C2IR LearnNet, IE 101, "Institutional Effectiveness" Topic 2, Lesson 1. Gainesville: University of Florida, 2008c.

Malone, P. R. "Institutional Effectiveness Practices in Colleges and Universities in the Southeastern United States." Unpublished doctoral dissertation, Florida State University, 2003. Retrieved February 11, 2011 from http://etd.lib.fsu.edu/theses/available/etd-11142003-170546/unrestricted/01diss.pdf.pdf.

McLeod, M. W., and Atwell, C. A. "A Mini-Dictionary on Institutional Effectiveness Terms." *Community College Review,* 1992, *20*(2), 30–38.

Muffo, J. "Institutional Effectiveness, Student Learning, and Outcomes Assessment." In R. Howard (ed.), *Institutional Research: Decision Support in Higher Education.* Tallahassee, Fla.: Association for Institutional Research, 2001.

National Commission on Excellence in Education. *A Nation at Risk: The Imperative for Educational Reform.* Washington, D.C.: National Commission on Excellence in Education, 1983. http://www.mat.uc.pt/~emsa/PMEnsino/ANationatRisk.pdf.

Rogers, J. T. "Assessment in Accreditation: Has It Made a Difference?" *Assessment Update,* 1997, *9*(4), 1–2, 15.

Rossman, J. E., and El-Khawas, E. *Thinking About Assessment: Perspectives for Presidents and Chief Academic Officers.* Washington, D.C.: American Council on Education and American Association for Higher Education, 1987.

Southern Association for Colleges and Schools. *Criteria for Accreditation.* Retrieved from http://www.utm.edu/organizations/sacs/criteria3.html on February 1, 2011.

RONALD B. HEAD *serves as a special projects officer at Tidewater Community College in Norfolk, Virginia; teaches doctoral education courses online for the University of Phoenix; and does consulting work in accreditation and institutional effectiveness.*

2

Institutional effectiveness is defined in light of the requirements of the six regional accrediting agencies, common terms are delineated, and the processes and practice of institutional effectiveness in community colleges is explored.

Institutional Effectiveness as Process and Practice in the American Community College

Terri Mulkins Manning

The six regional accrediting agencies in the United States have created a set of standards based on best practices in colleges and universities. The evolving perception of an effective institution is one that uses data, assessment, and evaluation results to improve programs and services and strives for a high level of institutional quality. While the regional accrediting agencies require institutional effectiveness (IE) within colleges and universities, institutions need to recognize the value of IE in transforming institutional culture and focusing attention on student success and institutional improvement. Colleges that participate in IE as a function of compliance do not reap the benefits that colleges that use it as an institutional change agent do.

Institutional effectiveness is a term that has been around for more than twenty-five years, and although there are commonalities among the regional accrediting agencies, no single agreed-on definition exists. Some specifically define *institutional effectiveness*, while others address the processes and practices expected of colleges through the reaffirmation process. One common strand across all six agencies is the high proportion of colleges receiving recommendations in the institutional effectiveness areas (for example, assessment, program and learning outcomes, and general education competencies). Because this chapter's focus is on the processes and practices typically included in institutional effectiveness, I define

New Directions for Community Colleges, no. 153, Spring 2011 © 2011 Wiley Periodicals, Inc.
Published online in Wiley Online Library (wileyonlinelibrary.com) • DOI: 10.1002/cc.433

institutional effectiveness as consisting of a set of ongoing and systematic institutional processes and practices that include planning, the evaluation of programs and services, the identification and measurement of outcomes across all institutional units (including learning outcomes in instructional programs), and the use of data and assessment results to inform decision making. All of these activities are accomplished with the purpose of improving programs and services and improving student success and institutional quality.

If there is one characteristic that is common among all six regional accrediting agencies, it is that the mandate for IE requires that colleges be purposeful in their planning. All six regional agencies require colleges to identify their predetermined outcomes for students and address ways all college units assist in creating an environment conducive to and in support of learning. To create an IE culture and atmosphere, one that permeates the institution (all people, processes, and practices), some key terms from the definition I have provided need further explanation:

- *Ongoing* means more than one rotation of a given process or practice. Colleges keep the momentum going from the previous accreditation site visit and do not attempt to gear up one year before the next one by running the entire college through some evaluative process so they can be ready for a visiting team. *Ongoing*, when addressing processes, means cyclical. When colleges view IE as a culturally transforming process that can be used for many purposes, faculty and administrators begin to rely on its ongoing nature.
- *Systematic* means that the institution defines and creates an organized IE system. Systems can typically be mapped out with a time line, an information flow, and an approval chain. IE systems are integrated and synergistic in nature.
- *Institutional* means common agreement across the institution that these processes are the institution's processes. Because of the politics within institutions, colleges can face minirevolutions within departments over the issues of learning outcomes assessment. Offshoots arise from one department or unit that can lead to many other offshoots, and soon colleges find themselves with a disconnected, unfocused set of initiatives that cannot be brought together with a central focus. Colleges should adopt consistent, inclusive, and effective processes and practices; agree on them across the institution; exempt no one; and disallow unsanctioned, disconnected attempts. Institutional effectiveness processes should be carried out as a single uniform institutional effort. The formation of an IE team or committee and an institutional IE plan can help keep this to a minimum.
- *Evaluation* implies answering several questions. "Did the program work the way we anticipated it would work?" "Did students accomplish what we expected them to accomplish [knowledge, behaviors, attitudes,

skills, and so forth]?" "Did the administrative unit deliver what it claimed it would deliver?" Good evaluation assesses progress along the way, analyzes that progress, and informs programmatic direction, change, and improvement. It also measures the overall effectiveness of the program, course, or service. Evaluation is exact, well defined, and planned.

- *Outcomes* are benefits for the recipients. The recipients of courses, programs, and student services are students. The benefits students receive are increases in their knowledge and skills, changed attitudes and values, improved conditions and status, and increased opportunities. Student outcomes can be recognized immediately or throughout the life of a student. They can be measured at any point within a course, during a capstone course, at graduation, or at any point after the student leaves the college. Measuring student outcomes (learning, program, or institutional) takes time and resources, two things most institutions lack beyond one year after graduation. Multiple types of outcomes are assessed within colleges and universities. Some of these are mentioned by specific accrediting agencies and require further definitions:

  Learning outcomes are changes observed or measured within students that result from the learning that takes place in the classroom or through classroom activities such as reading, homework assignments, and group projects. Learning outcomes can be general in nature, such as improving critical thinking skills, or specific to a discipline, such as nursing students' improving their ability to take accurate blood pressure readings.

  Program outcomes are benefits students receive as a result of the entire program of study. They are most easily defined by asking program faculty one question: "Are there any benefits program completers receive or gain that students who take only a few courses do not?" Typically program completion leads to passing licensure exams and better employment opportunities, but also to a deeper knowledge of the content field, commitment to lifelong learning, and greater satisfaction from working in the field. Complex concepts are often covered in multiple courses, and students cannot demonstrate mastery until their capstone course or comprehensive exam.

  Institutional outcomes are benefits institutions want for all of their students regardless of major. These types of outcomes often relate to the general education core set of courses and the college-level competencies institutions want students to achieve. But institutional outcomes can be different based on the mission of the institution (for example, theological seminaries and religious schools) and the student body served.

  Administrative outcomes are benefits to faculty, staff, or students due to the purpose and function of administrative units and support services. Departments and units can establish outcomes for themselves, such as counseling wanting to recruit and hire a new bilingual counselor to expand services for students (the college would benefit from this inclusion). Campus security, for example, may desire that all college constituents feel safe while on campus, so security staff upgrade lighting and add safety and security training through professional development. When surveyed, faculty, staff, and students rate their perceptions of safety as very high. These types of outcomes are critical to IE and look at the effectiveness and efficiency of all areas of the college.

- *Using data to inform decision making* has received a lot of attention over the past few years as colleges and universities strive to create a "culture of evidence" at their institutions. This implies that administrators, faculty, and frontline staff make decisions based not on anecdotal information but on student success data, outcomes assessment results, and feedback to inform decision making. Units do not use anecdotal information to make decisions but instead request information from the institutional research (IR) office or information technology staff to determine college and student needs.
- *Improving student success and institutional quality* requires that an institution define "student success and quality" and create a set of benchmarks or measures to show improvement over time. This begins with a data-gathering phase when the college community is asked, "If we improve institutional quality, what would we observe?" and, "If we improve student learning and success, what can we measure?" Some typical indicators might be incremental increases in term-to-term retention, graduation and transfer rates, successful course completion, and credit hours completed.

Reporting Structure for Institutional Effectiveness

Most community colleges have an institutional research, planning and research, or IE unit, which is typically a one-person office with some administrative support. One study found that approximately 50 percent of community colleges had small IR offices, with one full-time or part-time person (Morest & Jenkins, 2007). When the mandate for assessing student learning outcomes came down from the accrediting agencies, the IR office found itself overwhelmed by the complexity of the task. Because the task was large and the staff small, many institutions developed a committee and process structure that helped colleges get the work done. Some IR or IE offices report directly to the president and others to the chief academic or administrative officer. Wherever the office reports, one thing is clear: IR or IE staff find themselves in the position of needing to motivate people who do not report to them and to do things they do not want to do and for no clear reward.

NEW DIRECTIONS FOR COMMUNITY COLLEGES • DOI: 10.1002/cc

Processes for Institutional Effectiveness

Because IE is an institution-wide, integrated, and ongoing set of processes, forming an institutional effectiveness committee (IEC) is an effective way of ensuring participation and responsibility across the college (see Figure 2.1). Institutional research staff members often feel underpowered in regard to requiring assessment and evaluation participation from all college staff. But a well-formed IE committee, given the charge and complete support of the president, can garner greater participation from across the college. Institutional effectiveness committees can be large or small and can serve as the umbrella or oversight group for all work related to student learning outcomes, strategic planning, and program and unit review.

The IEC can be a powerful committee that includes carefully selected opinion leaders from across the college and takes on important functions. It can be responsible for the development of an outcome matrix for the institution to include institutional outcomes (learning for students and other issues such as professional development for faculty and staff). The committee can work alone or with the assistance of community forums, surveys, and focus groups. Committee members gather data on institutional quality indicators

Figure 2.1. Responsibilities of the Institutional
Effectiveness Committee

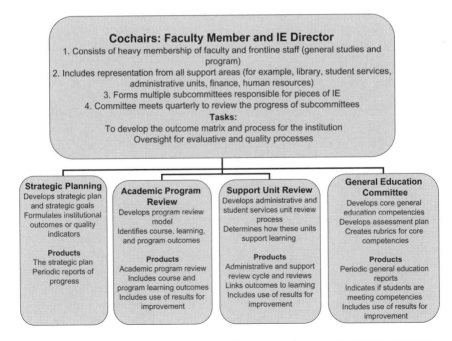

and determine how administrative and student services units support learning. The IEC can facilitate the development of all college evaluative processes such as program and unit reviews, the assessment of general education competencies, and strategic planning. While the accrediting agencies see IE as consisting of planning, evaluation, and assessment, the strategic planning committee at some community colleges is the larger committee and the IEC is a subcommittee of strategic planning. Regardless of the title of the larger committee, subcommittees can be formed to accomplish several tasks at the college—for example:

- *The strategic planning committee* responsible for developing the strategic plan (with collegewide input and support), the strategic goals, and annual priorities; developing institutional quality indicators and outcomes; and measuring periodic progress toward the goals. Products delivered by the strategic planning committee would include the strategic plan, the strategic goals, benchmarks to periodically measure progress toward institutional outcomes or quality indicators, and annual priorities for the institution.
- *The academic or instructional program review committee* responsible for developing an evaluative process for academic programs and departments. This subcommittee would be responsible for developing the program review model for the institution and identifying course, learning, and program outcomes for each area (with the strong participation of program faculty). Products delivered by this subcommittee would include the academic program review model (including the identification, assessment methods, and results of outcomes assessment), the calendar and time line (cycle), and the identified strategies for improvement or change as a result of the evaluative and assessment process.
- *Support unit review committee* (administrative and student services areas) responsible for developing the administrative and student services unit review process. This subcommittee would be responsible for identifying outcomes in all noninstructional areas (with the participation of staff in each area) and determining ways to link unit effectiveness to support of student learning. Products delivered would include the administrative and support services review process and cycle and the use of results to improve programs and services.
- *The general education committee* would contain faculty from the general education areas of the college and some program faculty to address expected outcomes from the general education core courses. This subcommittee would be responsible for creating a list of core general education competencies and a minimum standard students must obtain, assisting in the development of assessment tools and grading rubrics, and developing an effective cyclical process for measuring the competencies. The products delivered by this subcommittee would be periodic

NEW DIRECTIONS FOR COMMUNITY COLLEGES • DOI: 10.1002/cc

general education reports, faculty analysis of the results of assessment, and a plan for improving student success.

Colleges often find that in order to support IE processes, they have to focus some attention on assessment methods. Strategic planning committees may be mostly concerned with assessing institutional-level outcomes, a program review committee may be more concerned with program outcomes, and a general education committee may focus mostly on course-level learning outcomes. Regardless of the level of outcomes, good assessment techniques and products need to be delivered. The most important aspect of assessment is not that "we have done it" but that "we have used the results of it to inform action." Colleges should consider some of the following:

- Classroom-based or embedded assessments allow faculty to start with what they are already doing or develop an assessment tool that supports learning in the classroom.
- Formative evaluation of teaching (mostly of interest to new faculty) is gaining attention as a way to assess progress on learning outcomes over the term rather than the summative tools most institutions collect after the term is over, too late for faculty to address identified student issues.
- Student surveys (national or home grown) ask questions related to attitudes and behaviors of students (not self-assessments of how much they have learned).
- Qualitative methods such as focus groups, interviews, or SWOT (strengths, weaknesses, opportunities, threats) analyses can accumulate important data to determine program direction and barriers to student success.
- Benchmarking (internally against the college's previous performance or against an external group of colleges) provides colleges with important comparative information.
- Faculty-staff surveys allow administrative units to ask outcome-based questions to determine the attainment of administrative outcomes.

The Cyclical Nature of Institutional Effectiveness

Because IE processes and activities are carried out with the purpose of improving programs and services and increasing student success and institutional quality, they are cyclical in nature. Assessments and evaluations are completed and analyzed, and then strategies for change are implemented. Because implementing improvement strategies and then observing change takes time, programs are reevaluated every few years (the average time between reviews is two to five years). The nature and timing of the cycle can be different based on the size and program composition of the college. Larger institutions may have over one hundred programs or units that participate in program review, and their students may complete programs on average in four to six years. Putting programs on a five-year revolving cycle may therefore be best for that institution. Institutions that have participated in program review for multiple cycles are able to observe changes and improvements over time. A key to an effective cycle is giving the programs or units adequate time to reflect, make changes, and see the impact of those changes. Some colleges require an annual follow-up to program or unit review until the program reenters the cycle. Creating a cycle where one group of programs or units is reviewed every year on a revolving three- to five-year cycle keeps the college continuously involved in institutional improvement.

Getting Started with Institutional Effectiveness at Community Colleges

While colleges in many regions of the country have been working with IE process and practices for decades, other are new to the process. Colleges often feel overwhelmed by the comprehensive and inclusive nature of IE and have trouble getting started. Colleges can consider the following steps when beginning this important and institution-changing work:

1. Communicate the purpose of IE to the college community. Faculty and staff need to know not only the importance of IE for accreditation but also as a way to focus energy and attention on student learning and institutional improvement.
2. Provide professional development on the concepts of IE, defining and assessing student learning outcomes, and using results to improve institutional quality. This ensures that all faculty and staff have a common knowledge and vocabulary as they begin the work.
3. Obtain open and strong administrative support for institutional improvement. This often involves staff time and funding to support the processes.
4. Seek broad engagement in the development of evaluative processes and practices. Get as much faculty and frontline staff participation as possible to gain support and ownership of the processes. This should not be a top-down process driven by administrative agendas.
5. If faculty and staff are expected to use results to improve programs and services, administrators need to read and respond to the reviews and evaluations in an honest and supportive way. If resources are needed to improve or expand programs, administrators must be committed to supporting the recommendations with needed resources. Otherwise faculty will recognize IE as just one more academic exercise that results in faculty work and no result.
6. Put the time and resources needed into tracking processes. "The devil is in the details" is never truer than with IE. Once the faculty have defined

outcomes and created the assessment process, the difficult work begins. Questions arise that must be answered, or progress can slow to a crawl or be destroyed altogether. When are assessments delivered? Who collects them? Who scores them? Where do we send the results? What do we do with all the data? Create a flowchart for each process with time lines that help keep people on track.

Conclusion

When a college creates an IE model and set of practices that fit and support its culture and priorities, transformation can occur. Because community colleges are active places with overworked faculty and staff, the tendency of faculty and staff is often to look at what a similar institution is doing and replicate it. But colleges should create processes and practices around the priorities and needs of their own students, staff, community, and state and regional mandates. Institutional effectiveness is a way colleges keep their finger on the pulse of student needs and their eye on institutional quality. Time spent on developing useful and meaningful processes and practices will have great payoff in the end.

Reference

Morest, V., and Jenkins, D. *Institutional Research and the Culture of Evidence at Community Colleges.* New York: Community College Research Center, Teachers College, Columbia University, 2007.

TERRI MULKINS MANNING is associate vice president of institutional research at Central Piedmont Community College in Charlotte, North Carolina.

NEW DIRECTIONS FOR COMMUNITY COLLEGES • DOI: 10.1002/cc

3

Heightened national goals for degree attainment in the United States means increasing prominence for community colleges, which entails greater scrutiny in the form of accountability. Technology and a new generation of accountability measures appropriate to the distinctive community college mission are available to meet this challenge.

Accountability and Institutional Effectiveness in the Community College

Peter T. Ewell

The accountability dimension of institutional effectiveness has been an explicit concern of community colleges since the Southern Association of Colleges and Schools (SACS) adopted it as a review criterion in 1986 (Rogers, 1997; Ewell, 2008). Popularly known at that time as "the full employment act for institutional research," similar provisions were in place at all six regional accreditation commissions by the end of the decade. As originally envisioned, institutional effectiveness was intended to be applied to all aspects of an institution's operations. This distinguished it from assessment, a term that rose to prominence at about the same time but was largely confined to student learning and development. The late 1980s was also a period of significant accountability activity on the part of state governments, which quickly embraced institutional effectiveness concepts and language when they developed statistical performance indicators and, in some cases, associated performance funding schemes.

During this period, the community college sector was prominent in developing ways to respond to the challenge of measuring institutional effectiveness. The first edition of *Core Indicators of Effectiveness for Community Colleges*, for example, was issued in 1994 and has remained in print ever since, through several ups and downs of state and accreditation interest in accountability for student success (American Association of Community Colleges, 1994; Alfred, Ewell, Hudgins, and McClenney, 1999). But beginning with the much highlighted deliberations of the Secretary's Commission

NEW DIRECTIONS FOR COMMUNITY COLLEGES, no. 153, Spring 2011 © 2011 Wiley Periodicals, Inc.
Published online in Wiley Online Library (wileyonlinelibrary.com) • DOI: 10.1002/cc.434

on the Future of Higher Education (popularly known as the Spellings Commission), the past five years have spurred lively interest in the topic. More specifically the experience of the Spellings Commission prompted higher education leaders to adopt a more proactive stance with respect to accountability (Association of American Colleges and Universities and Council for Higher Education Accreditation, 2008). The Voluntary System of Accountability, a performance reporting template developed jointly by the American Association of State Colleges and Universities and the Association of Public Land-Grant Universities, and the New Leadership Alliance for Student Learning and Accountability were among its early products. Two years later, a coalition of community college organizations began work on its own response, the Voluntary Framework of Accountability (VFA), which is intended to compile information for external consumers on various measures of institutional effectiveness in an easily accessible fashion (American Association of Community Colleges, 2011).

This new wave of attention to institutional effectiveness on the part of community colleges, moreover, emerged in an altered environment with respect to the technical ability to calculate the kinds of comparative measures of performance that realizing the concept of institutional effectiveness requires. Powerful new databases now enable students to be tracked over time, through multiple institutional settings, and into the workforce. At the same time, many new instruments and methodologies for gathering evidence of student academic achievement have emerged. These developments have in some ways eased the task for community colleges that are attempting to respond to escalating demands to evaluate institutional effectiveness. But by defining new limits to what is possible, they may have also helped fuel the demand for new measures in the first place.

This chapter sketches emerging trends in the accountability dimension of institutional effectiveness for community colleges by reviewing the motives of the various players and their specific accountability interests in community colleges, describing the challenges that community colleges face in responding to these demands, and elaborating on some new directions that have emerged in accountability reporting over the past few years for community college systems and institutions.

External Accountability Players

It has become commonplace in discussions of accountability in higher education to frame the topic in terms of the entity that must demonstrate accountability and that which requires it, together with the domain of performance or action for which accountability is called for—in short, "Who owes what to whom?" (State Higher Education Executive Officers, 2005). Answers to this apparently simple question have always been complex for community colleges, and because of recent changes in the political and economic landscape, they have changed over time. Principal accountability players are discussed in this section roughly in the order in which they influence community colleges (although this may vary by state and individual college mission) and include states, the federal government, accreditors, service regions and employers, and various third-party players.

States.   Community colleges are public institutions that receive significant amounts of state support. And although overall levels of state subsidy per student may be lower for community colleges than for their public four-year counterparts, they also tend to receive greater proportions of their overall revenue from state sources. This means that states, acting as investors and shareholders, have strong accountability relationships with community colleges in the domains of efficient operations and results achieved. This relationship is amplified for the many community colleges that are parts of systems under governing board authority. Here the state's role is that of owner-operator—not only a source of support but with an oversight responsibility for specific policies, rules, and regulations as well.

As a second accountability obligation to states, community colleges are expected to serve as an integral part of a larger statewide educational pipeline, yielding baccalaureate graduates through their transfer links with four-year institutions. This assigned role brings with it obligations to prepare students for four-year transfer and to maintain or increase the proportion who do so. At least as important, a prominent expectation of community colleges is to address state workforce needs by developing cross-cutting skills like problem solving and teamwork and, in the vast majority of community colleges that offer occupational programs, preparation for specific occupations to meet the state's current and anticipated workforce demands. Increasingly undergirding both the workforce preparation and transfer functions, moreover, are needs to address deficiencies in the preparation of entering students. Finally, a number of community college systems (for example, in North Carolina and Washington) have additional assignments in the areas of Adult Basic Instruction, English as a Second Language, and General Educational Development.

The Federal Government.   Traditionally the federal government has played a more distant role than the states in funding community colleges and holding them accountable for specific performance. As substantial participants in federal student aid programs, of course, community colleges fall under the same kinds of scrutiny to serve as effective stewards of federal dollars that affect all institutions that participate in these programs. But for the most part, the responsibility for ensuring that these accountability obligations are discharged is delegated to federally approved accreditation organizations. An exception is community colleges that operate federal programs directly—for example, literacy programs, Workforce Investment Act (WIA) initiatives, or Carl Perkins programs—with additional specific performance and performance reporting obligations.

In the past couple of years, federal interest in community college performance has increased markedly. The Obama administration's ambitious access goal of matching global attainment rates of 60 percent of a young adult age cohort with a college credential by 2025 will fall disproportionately on the nation's community college sector. This increased salience is recognized in the unprecedented number of senior U.S. Department of Education appointments drawn from community college backgrounds. On top of this are categorical programs in the various stimulus packages that number in the billions of dollars. If these efforts bear fruit, they will assuredly come at an additional price with respect to federal accountability.

Accreditation.   Accreditation operates in a dual role with respect to community college accountability. As noted, it stands in for the federal government in ensuring that institutions that receive financial aid funds have the administrative capacity to house and disburse them properly. Over the years, this basic accountability lever for fiscal matters has been gradually extended to include additional oversight in areas such as degree program specifications, definitions of instructional time, and student complaint systems. At a more fundamental level, accreditation has served as the principal external means to ensure institutional quality in U.S. higher education for more than a hundred years.

Seeking and earning accreditation would be essential for community colleges, even without the federal connection, because it constitutes the generally accepted public seal of approval that an institution meets acceptable quality standards. Recently, meeting accreditation standards has become more challenging because of increased expectations with respect to the assessment of student learning outcomes. This too is in part a result of the federal connection; since 1990, the U.S. Department of Education has established and enforced progressively higher standards on institutional accreditors in their recognition processes. But regardless of cause, the contribution of accreditation to the mélange of forces calling on community colleges for more and better evidence of student academic achievement, together with evidence that institutions are actually using this evidence to make improvements, is substantial.

Regions and Employers.   Community colleges are in essence regional service providers, responsible primarily for delivering education and training to citizens and organizations within a defined geographical region. Although many community colleges are state funded and governed, this community service focus remains at the forefront and is a broad foundation for accountability. For other community colleges, accountability relationships with the surrounding community are direct, embodied in elected local boards and tax support, and constituents expect appropriate return on investment. At the same time, many community colleges provide direct services to regional employers in the form of short-term contract training and employee literacy training; although these are market driven, and in this sense self-regulating, they automatically entail an additional dimension of stakeholder accountability. Finally, community college effectiveness is

NEW DIRECTIONS FOR COMMUNITY COLLEGES • DOI: 10.1002/cc

sometimes seen as embodied in the institution's financial contributions to the region, visible in employment opportunities and economic impact.

The "Third Estate". Largely missing from the roster of accountability players affecting community colleges two decades ago, the press and third-party policy organizations have now joined the ranks of those that institutions need to consider in terms of performance. A major actor here is the Community College Survey of Student Engagement (CCSSE), which began operations in 2001. The CCSSE is a widely regarded indicator of performance in the realms of student engagement and the effectiveness of retention and completion practices, and institutional results are publicly available on the CCSSE Web site. Although these results are not arrayed in tabular form so they can be directly compared across institutions, this has not prevented some organizations and the trade press in higher education from making these comparisons At the same time, community college organizations themselves are being much more proactive about holding the entire sector accountable through efforts like the VFA. As transparency becomes an increasingly prominent feature of the higher education landscape, leaders of community colleges should expect more such third-party accountability players to be added to the traditional array.

Defining Effectiveness: Challenges to Community Colleges

Community colleges are among the most distinctive types of institutions in American postsecondary education. Largely as a result, they are ill served by the kinds of performance measures that are typically used in determining institutional effectiveness. There are many legitimate reasons for this, and it is important for both policymakers and institutional leaders to understand them so they can argue for, and develop, more appropriate measures.

Multiple Missions. Comprehensive community colleges provide a variety of quite different functions simultaneously:

- The first two years of a baccalaureate degree
- Associate degree instruction in many vocational fields that also carries transfer credit
- Terminal occupational credentialing that has immediate workplace value (both associate level and certification) but does not carry transfer credit
- Remedial and developmental instruction to render students college ready
- Noncredit instruction such as literacy training and English as a Second Language
- Contract training for employers and local businesses

Added to this, in some cases, are professional baccalaureate programs at one end of the scale and personal development and recreational education classes open to citizens of the region at the other end. Not only are these different functions offered simultaneously at many colleges, they also operate more or less independently of one another. This has led some to describe the comprehensive community college not as an institution but as a "holding company"—a legal and administrative entity supervising a series of quite different "businesses," each with its own leadership and respective business model (Ewell, 1994).

This multimission character poses significant challenges to the application of traditional conceptions of institutional effectiveness to community colleges because these tend to assume a unitary institutional mission that defines what it means to be effective. The established answer, and the model proposed by the original *Core Indicators of Effectiveness for Community Colleges*, is to develop a distinct line of performance measures tailored directly to each mission dimension. But this misses at least two important institution-level areas of performance. One is strategic leadership and planning, including institutional research. Evaluating effectiveness here is not only important for the institution's future in a changing environment, but is also a particular and growing concern of accreditors. A second critical area of collective performance is enrollment management. Because of the kinds of students they serve, community colleges are especially challenged by retention and degree completion. Ten years of experience drawn from intensive efforts to improve student success, like Achieving the Dream, suggest that integrated, institution-wide student success programs that include directed placement, mandatory advising, early warning systems, and "one-stop-shopping" for student services are far better than a range of piecemeal services. These are areas of performance that need to be looked at from an institution-wide point of view, even as the effectiveness of distinct academic and service programs offered by the various parts of the "holding company" is examined independently.

Distinctive and Diverse Patterns of Attendance. Community college leaders have long claimed that established measures of student progression like the Graduation Rate Survey (GRS) required by the Integrated Postsecondary Educational Data System are not appropriate to their institutions. This is because the GRS calculation is based on tracking an entering student cohort of full-time, first-time-in-college students through a relatively short tracking period (now 200 percent of the catalogue length of the program) to the completion of a degree or credential at the same college.

For the typical comprehensive community college, there are at least four things wrong with this approach. First, entering students may have had some (and sometimes substantial) postsecondary enrollment experience somewhere else. Second, many beginning students enroll for less than a full-time load in their first term and maintain this lighter load throughout their academic career. Third, as a result of continuous part-time attendance, the 200 percent time window allowed for completing a degree may be too short.[1] Fourth, the degree that a student eventually earns after entering a particular community college may be actually earned at another institution.[2] In combination, these four limitations mean that the proportion of students who can be included in the GRS graduation rate calculation at many community colleges is less than 15 percent of total enrollment.

A related challenge that cuts across these technical defects of progression measures is the question of student intent. Community college critics of established student progression measures frequently claim that such measures do not take into account the fact that many of their entering students do not intend to earn a degree. Alternative measures designed to take this into account generally start the tracking clock only after a specified number of credits have already been earned. For example, the Florida Community College System reports completion rates on the basis of students who have earned at least fifteen credits. But this is not really satisfactory because no one can know how many degree-intending students withdrew before attaining the established credit threshold for starting the tracking period. And many students within this group are de facto degree seeking by virtue of their receipt of federal financial aid. Asking students about their intent has been tried many times as a potential way to address this difficulty. But response rates can be spotty and student answers unreliable because to declare oneself to be a nondegree student shuts off potential access to financial aid. The only viable way to handle these difficulties may be to report multiple statistics, carefully defined, and let consumers make the judgment (Ewell, 2009).

Broad Range of Student Characteristics.   Finally, community colleges enroll a wide variety of students whose performance in terms of a single set of defined success criteria can legitimately vary significantly. With respect to entering preparation and academic ability, for instance, they cover the gamut. Differing intents and enrollment behaviors can yield equally varied patterns of success. And community college enrollments are easily the most varied among postsecondary sectors with respect to demographic diversity and socioeconomic background. One result is that the kinds of central tendency statistics usually used in accountability-oriented institutional effectiveness reporting schemes do not tell stakeholders very much. An average graduation rate of 22 percent at a given college may vary from more than two-thirds for well-prepared and application-screened nursing or allied health students to less than 19 percent for undeclared students.

Careful disaggregation in reporting institutional effectiveness measures that apply to students is frequently called for (Ewell, 2008). Breaking results down by important population groups not only gives accountability stakeholders a much better picture of what is really going on inside a given institution but also allows potential "customers" to see what the college's record has been with students "like them," with particular sets of advantages and disadvantages. The best kinds of disaggregation, moreover, may not be obvious. Most community college fact books, for example, break down descriptive and performance statistics one variable at a time—male or female, full time or part time, by academic program, and so on. Instead, the most revealing differences may be across student subpopulations defined in terms of particular combinations of variables—for example, full-time women enrolled in selective allied health programs who did not require remediation, or Hispanic men with no declared major beginning at the lowest placement level in mathematics. All institutions have not one "student body" but many, and community colleges tend to have the greatest diversity in this respect.

*   *   *

While these challenges to applying established concepts of institutional effectiveness to community colleges are real, they also apply to individual colleges within the sector to varying degrees. Some community colleges are primarily transfer institutions with large numbers of traditionally aged students attending full time. Others are primarily engaged in part-time or short-course vocational training. Still others embody all the varied characteristics that yield the measurement challenges discussed. Leaders of individual institutions, with the advice of their institutional research offices, need to carefully determine who they are with respect to their salient characteristics before adopting any standard set of institutional effectiveness measures for accountability reporting purposes. And if such measures are mandated, they should undertake to report more than just what is asked for in order to convey a true picture of performance.

Emerging Remedies

The growing importance of accountability for institutional effectiveness, the existence of myriad stakeholders to whom accountability is owed, and the continuing challenges of applying traditional concepts of institutional effectiveness to the distinctive world of the community college are giving rise to new practices. Some of these are the result of genuinely fresh thinking, while others are extensions of established tools or concepts. Most have been made possible by significant advances in the technology surrounding student records systems and assessment. Indeed, many of the measures proposed twenty years ago that were not possible or feasible then have become not only practicable but common. This section is not intended to provide an exhaustive catalogue of such practices. Indeed, any such list would probably be obsolete before this volume is published. The intent instead is to illustrate the kinds of practices that are emerging in accountability reporting in some of the most prominent areas of institutional effectiveness reporting.

Student Progression.   Retention, program completion, transfer, and job placement have always been high on the list of institutional effectiveness domains for community colleges. Graduation rates were among the first three indicators on the original list of *Core Indicators of Community College Effectiveness* (Alfred, Ewell, Hudgins, and McClenney, 1999), and their progeny in the form of a growing array of more sophisticated student success measures remain at the top of the list today. Partly this is because of the now-urgent national goal to raise degree attainment rates among young adults. But partly it is because retention and degree completion rates can also be seen as summative measures of institutional productivity—one of the reasons that graduation rates are the only measure entirely common across public institutions in all states (Burke and Minnassians, 2003).

What is different about student progression measures today as compared to a decade ago? One powerful conceptual breakthrough is the notion of the educational pipeline—the seamless progression of students through high school, into college, through postsecondary study (frequently involving multiple institutions), and into the workforce (National Center for Public Policy in Higher Education, 2004). Stimulated by *Measuring Up 2000* (National Center for Public Policy in Higher Education, 2000), the fifty-state "report card" for higher education published by the National Center for Public Policy in Higher Education and the policy work of the National Center for Higher Education Management Systems in the late 1990s, many states established policies focused on analyzing "flow" through the pipeline and specific kinds policy remedies to address identified "leaks" and "bottlenecks" (Ewell, Boeke, and Zis, 2008). And this was part of a widespread shift in the posture of accountability from managing institutional behavior toward emphasizing higher education's benefits to citizens of the state (Ewell and Jones, 2006). One of the most prominent of these policy transformations was in Kentucky, which simultaneously restructured its two-year college system from branch campuses of the University of Kentucky to an integrated system of community and technical colleges, with a new set of state and institutional performance indicators organized around four goals for higher education–centered citizen benefits.

Accompanying this conceptual shift are two technical advances that make new measures possible. The first is the rapid development and integration of state longitudinal data systems based on student unit record (SUR) databases. Forty-two of the fifty states now have such systems, and both their data contents and state facility with using them are growing rapidly (Ewell and Boeke, 2007). Significant infusions of resources on the part of the federal government through State Longitudinal Data System development grants issued in 2009 and additional dollars delivered through the federal stimulus package mean that these capabilities will get much better in the next decade. These enable students to be tracked across multiple institutions within a given state, enabling true transfer rates to be calculated and ultimate graduation rates to be enhanced. Data holdings of the National Student Clearinghouse, which are also expanding, can extend this reach to the nation as a whole. Clearinghouse data holdings now include more than 93 percent of the nation's postsecondary enrollments. A recent study found that on a national basis, ultimate graduation rates can be boosted almost 10 percent if students are followed to any institution in any state (National Center for Higher Education Management Systems, 2008).

Reaching further, postsecondary SURs can increasingly be linked with workforce data in the form of the Unemployment Insurance Wage Record files that states are required to maintain by the U.S. Department of Labor. Although the data contents of these files are limited and making the linkage is still awkward, at least twenty-three states have used these resources to automatically calculate job placement rates by field of study for program graduates and former students. This is good news for community college accountability because ultimate success in fulfilling mission goals such as transfer and job placement can be tracked regardless of destination and artificial time limits.

A second important development has been the creation of so-called intermediate progression measures. Community colleges are particularly challenged by the fact that small proportions of their enrollments complete programs of study and earn a degree. But many do reach identifiable attainment milestones short of a degree that are important for later success. Among these are particular levels of credit attainment (twelve- and thirty-semester credit equivalents are typically used), successful exit from developmental to college-level work, completion of one or more basic skills or literacy courses, or achievement of transfer-ready or work-ready status (Ewell, 2008). Transfer-ready status is usually defined as having completed thirty semester credits, passed English Composition and a college-level mathematics course, and completed at least one transferable college-level course in a science, a social science, and the humanities. Workforce-ready status is usually defined as having completed a particular identifiable block of courses short of a degree or certificate that demonstrably leads to a marketable skill in a particular area of employment.

These progression measures reflect the diversity of the community college mission much more fully than traditional graduation rates and are gradually being adopted as institutional effectiveness measures by state community college systems. For example, the State Board of Community and Technical Colleges in Washington used this approach to investigate student progression from Adult Basic Education programs well below college level into and through collegiate study and just launched a pioneering performance funding scheme in which institutions earn "momentum points" worth additional funding based on the number of students who reach established enrollment progression milestones (Prince and Jenkins, 2005).

Student Learning Outcomes.   Assessing student learning outcomes has always been a particular challenge for community colleges because of the lack of suitable instruments and settings for assessment. When the first systematic assessment programs began in the mid-1980s, they tended to rely on standardized measures like the ACT Assessment or the Graduate

Record Examination administered outside the classroom. Not only were such measures largely unsuited for community college curricula, but there was also nowhere to administer them. Mechanisms like "assessment days," in which residential college students were assembled for assessment sessions or students were tested in residence halls, were unavailable to community colleges, where the only regular and reliable point of contact with students was in individual classrooms. Today, however, community colleges have a new attention to both appropriate instrumentation and creating appropriate settings.

With respect to method, some of this progress has been due to the emergence of new assessments and the ability to aggregate existing measures. For the transfer or general education component of the curriculum, for example, task-based assessments like the Collegiate Learning Assessment (CLA) have joined more conventional tests like the ACT Collegiate Assessment of Academic Proficiency and the ETS Proficiency Profile as appropriate end-of-program assessments. A recent institutional survey reveals that 28 percent of community colleges are now using such measures, compared to a national average of 19 percent (Kuh and Ikenberry 2009). For the occupational or vocational component of the curriculum, the ACT Work Keys examination measures general practice skills benchmarked to hundreds of occupations and trades nationwide. On the occupational side of the curriculum, moreover, community college students in many fields must also sit for licensure examinations, whose scores can be aggregated and used as institutional effectiveness measures for accountability purposes. But the problem has always been to assemble these many test scores and develop meaningful aggregations. Now these problems are being overcome through a combination of technology and the establishment of reliable networks of information sharing among licensing agencies, and several state performance measure systems (for example, those of North Carolina and Tennessee) make use of them.

A different route to generating evidence of learning outcomes has been more exciting in many ways—embedding assessments in some of the assignments that students must complete in their regular course of study. This approach is much more authentic than standardized testing because it can be tailored to specific curricular specifications. At least as important, it virtually eliminates the student motivation problems associated with external assessments (like the CLA), which do not count. The difficulty has always been how to implement this approach. In order to be reliable, each assignment needs to be scored by faculty judges using well-designed rubrics or scoring guides. Then this entire array of dissimilar performances must be aggregated to yield interpretable indexes of performance aligned with learning outcomes statements.

For many years, efforts to implement such approaches consumed enormous amounts of faculty time and produced unprecedented mounds of paper. Once again, though, rapid advances in technology have begun to make possible what was unwieldy and nearly unworkable a decade ago. For example, the eLumen approach, developed and tested by a consortium of community colleges in Minnesota and now available for adoption by any institution, has proven both effective and efficient in realizing the course-embedded approach.

Measures of Good Practice.   A third area in which considerable progress has been made in the past decade is measuring practices that community colleges engage in that are demonstrably related to learning and student success. This has been largely due to widespread adoption of the Community College Survey of Student Engagement (CCSSE). The CCSSE grew out of the earlier National Survey of Student Engagement, whose content was based on questions tapping institutional practices and student behaviors of demonstrated effectiveness in the research literature. CCSSE extended this conceptual coverage by also including items related to good practices leading to improved retention and program completion. The battery has recently been augmented by the Survey of Entering Student Engagement, a survey administered to beginning community college students to guide early-enrollment program development and intervention. CCSSE benchmark scores are reported publicly on CCSSE's Web site and have been used extensively since the survey's inception in helping individual community colleges demonstrate institutional effectiveness as part of accreditation and as part of state accountability reporting systems.

Institutional Benchmarking.   A final important development for community colleges in the area of institutional effectiveness is interinstitutional benchmarking. Comparing colleges on a range of indicators (both input and output) had become relatively well established in the four-year sector by the mid-1990s, as evidenced by such efforts as the AAU Data Exchange, the Higher Education Data Sharing Consortium, and the Delaware Project (Dunn, 1989). But similar external benchmarking efforts eluded community colleges for a variety of reasons. One was the enormous diversity of the sector. To be meaningful, core benchmarking measures needed to be truly comparable or applied within the limits of well-drawn peer comparison groups. Another was the attitude of community college leaders who, burned by previous unfavorable (and inappropriate) comparisons between community colleges and other sectors, innately resisted these kinds of measures. Gradually, however, these obstacles have been overcome. The National Community College Benchmarking Project (NCCBP), based at Johnson County Community College in Kansas, was launched in 2004 and now includes 210 participating community colleges. These institutions share data on twenty-five benchmark measures ranging from minority participation rates to career program graduates' job placement rates. Like most other data-sharing consortia, results of the NCCBP are confidential, but institutions can access and use national results or results for groups of peer institutions. Like CCSSE results, this can yield powerful information with which to make a college's case for institutional effectiveness in an accountability context. And consistent with growing national calls for externally benchmarked measures of performance, many users of the NCCBP report that they now frequently use their benchmark data as part of accreditation review and in state reports (Drennon, Ash, and Gillman, 2009).

Conclusion

Heightened national goals for degree attainment in the United States means increasing prominence for community colleges and undoubtedly more resources and media attention. This new prominence will also entail more scrutiny in the form of accountability. Technology and a new generation of accountability measures appropriate to the distinctive community college mission are now available to meet this challenge. Community colleges should embrace these measures, adapt them to their own circumstances to meet legitimate calls for accountability, and use the resulting information to get even better.

Notes

1. A study recently completed by NCHEMS using data from the National Student Clearinghouse indicated continuing degree completion by entering community college students (half-time and above) well beyond the eight-year mark (NCHEMS, 2008).
2. This fairly common situation is doubly debilitating under GRS rules because neither institution gets to count the student as a success: the student was not "first time" at the institution granting the degree and did not earn a degree from the institution where he or she first enrolled.

References

Alfred, R., Ewell, P., Hudgins, J., and McClenney, K. *Core Indicators of Effectiveness for Community Colleges.* (2nd ed.) Washington, D.C.: Community College Press, 1999.

American Association of Community Colleges. *Community Colleges: Core Indicators of Effectiveness.* Washington, D.C.: Community College Press, 1994.

American Association of Community College. *What is the VFA?* Retrieved on February 1, 2011 from http://www.aacc.nche.edu/Resources/aaccprograms/vfa/Pages/default. aspx.

Association of American Colleges and Universities and Council for Higher Education Accreditation. *New Leadership for Student Learning and Accountability: A Statement of Principles, Commitment to Action.* Washington, D.C.: Association for American Colleges and Universities and Council for Higher Education Accreditation, 2008.

Burke, J. C., and Minnassians, H. *Performance Reporting: "Real" Accountability or Accountability "Lite"?* Albany: Rockefeller Institute of Government, State University of New York, 2003.

Drennon, M., Ash, M., and Gillman, P. "How NCCBP Data Contributes to AQIP Accreditation and Ensures Continuous Quality Improvement of Institutional Processes." National Benchmarking Conference, State Fair Community College, Sedalia, Missouri, June 23, 2009.

Dunn, J. A. "Electronic Media and Information Sharing." In P. T. Ewell (ed.), *Enhancing Information Use in Decision Making*. New Directions for Institutional Research, no. 64. San Francisco: Jossey-Bass, 1989.

Ewell, P. T. Student Unit Record Systems and Postsecondary Accountability: Exploiting Emerging Data Resources. In Kevin Carey and Mark Schneider (eds), Accountability in American Higher Education, New York: Palgrave-Macmillan, 2010, 121–140.

Ewell, P. T. "The Assessment Movement: Implications for Teaching and Learning." In T. O'Bannion and Associates, *Teaching and Learning in the Community College*. Washington, D.C.: American Association of Community Colleges, 1994.

Ewell, P. T. *Community College Data and Performance Measure Toolkit*. New York: Community College Research Center, Teachers College, Columbia University, 2008.

Ewell, P. T. "Student Unit Record Databases and Postsecondary Accountability: Exploiting Emerging Data Resources." Paper prepared for the American Enterprise Institute Conference, Nov. 17, 2009.

Ewell, P. T., and Boeke, M. *Critical Connections: Linking States' Unit Record Systems to Track Student Progress*. Indianapolis, Ind.: Lumina Foundation for Education, 2007.

Ewell, P. T., Boeke, M., and Zis, S. *State Policies on Student Transitions: Results of a Fifty-State Inventory*. Boulder, Colo.: National Center for Higher Education Management Systems, 2008.

Ewell, P. T., and Jones, D. P. "State-Level Accountability for Higher Education: On the Edge of a Transformation." In N. B. Shulock (ed.), *Practitioners on Making Accountability Work for the Public*. New Directions for Higher Education, no. 135. San Francisco: Jossey-Bass, 2006.

Kuh, G., and Ikenberry, S. "More Than You Think, Less Than We Need: Learning Outcomes Assessment." In *American Higher Education*. Champaign, Ill.: National Institute for Learning Outcomes Assessment, 2009.

The National Center for Public Policy and Higher Education, 2004. *Measuring Up 2000: The State-by-State Report Card for Higher Education*. Retrieved from http://measuringup.highereducation.org/2000/ on February 1, 2011.

National Center for Higher Education Management Systems (NCPPHE). *Creating State-Level Degree Completion Rates from a National Database: Results of an Exploratory Analysis*. Boulder, Colo.: National Center for Higher Education Management Systems, 2008.

National Center for Public Policy in Higher Education (NCPPHE). *The Educational Pipeline: Big Investment, Big Returns*. Oakland, Calif.: National Center for Public Policy in Higher Education, 2004.

National Center for Public Policy in Higher Education (NCPPHE). Measuring Up 2000: The State-By-State Report Card for Higher Education. San Jose, CA: National Center for Public Policy in Higher Education, 2000.

Prince, D., and Jenkins, D. *Building Pathways to Success for Low-Skill Adult Students: Lessons for Community College Policy and Practice from a Statewide Longitudinal Study*. New York: Community College Research Center, Teachers College, Columbia University, 2005.

Rogers, J. T. "Assessment in Accreditation: Has It Made a Difference?" *Assessment Update*, 1997, 9(4), 1–2, 15.

State Higher Education Executive Officers. *Accountability for Better Results: A National Imperative for Higher Education*. Boulder, Colo.: State Higher Education Executive Officers, 2005.

PETER T. EWELL *is the vice president of the National Center for Higher Education Management Systems in Boulder, Colorado.*

4

Effective community colleges use the accreditation process to provide a framework for strengthening the effectiveness of programs and services.

Accreditation and Its Influence on Institutional Effectiveness

Ronald B. Head, Michael S. Johnson

The term *institutional effectiveness* was developed in response to accreditation, and this emphasizes the large extent to which accreditation drives institutional effectiveness efforts on community college campuses. Although accreditation is often viewed as onerous or as a burdensome external requirement, it confers a number of benefits to an institution. It verifies compliance with certain predetermined, common standards of excellence; it can protect an institution from unwarranted criticism and, to the extent that the faculty is involved, provide the stimulus for the improvement of courses and programs; it promotes internal unity and cohesiveness; students are in an improved position when it comes to judging various institutions and programs; and a college or university may more accurately ascertain the value and equivalency of transfer credits. Finally, accreditation assists in meeting one of several potential criteria for obtaining federal funding and assistance.

There are two general types of accreditation. *Institutional accreditation* is the process by which institutions of higher education are evaluated as a whole with an eye toward their unity of purpose and the extent to which the sum of the parts complement the whole. *Programmatic accreditation* focuses on components—programs, courses of study, and sometimes individual courses—within the institution. In this chapter, we focus solely on one type of institutional accreditation, which is commonly referred to as *regional accreditation* because the U.S. Department of Education, as well as the Council for

New Directions for Community Colleges, no. 153, Spring 2011 © 2011 Wiley Periodicals, Inc.
Published online in Wiley Online Library (wileyonlinelibrary.com) • DOI: 10.1002/cc.435

37

Higher Education Accreditation (CHEA), recognizes six agencies that confer accreditation to colleges and universities in their respective regions of the United States and abroad: the Middle States Commission on Higher Education (MSCHE); the New England Association of Schools and Colleges, Commission on Institutions of Higher Education (CIHE); the North Central Association of Colleges and Schools, The Higher Learning Commission (HLC); the Northwest Commission on Colleges and Universities (NWCCU); the Southern Association of Colleges and Schools Commission on Colleges (SACSCOC); and the Western Association of Schools and Colleges (WASC). There are also national accreditors that offer institutional accreditation. The regional accreditors tend to cover a broader range of institutions. Our intent in this chapter is to briefly examine the institutional effectiveness requirements of each of the six agencies. This examination will:

- Provide a framework to begin examining accreditation in more detail and determine which requirements affect different community colleges throughout the United States
- Give readers a better understanding of the similarities and differences in the way regional accrediting agencies interpret and apply institutional effectiveness
- Help practitioners understand the importance accrediting agencies attach to both institutional effectiveness and institutional research
- Provide some helpful resources that are available at no cost from the six regional accrediting agencies
- Explore how one regional agency's (SACSCOC) accreditation standards can be used to strengthen institutions through the institutional effectiveness process

Middle States Commission on Higher Education

Institutional effectiveness pervades *Characteristics of Excellence in Higher Education: Eligibility Requirements and Standards for Accreditation* (Middle States Commission on Higher Education, 2009), the document listing accreditation standards for the Middle States Commission on Higher Education. Indeed, a community college is required to "assess both institutional effectiveness and student learning outcomes, and use the results for improvement" (p. iv). Middle States, like all of the other regional agencies, is not prescriptive when it comes to implementing and assessing institutional effectiveness at institutions. As it notes:

> While the Commission expects institutions to assess institutional effectiveness, it does not prescribe a specific approach or methodology. The institution is responsible for determining its expected goals and the objectives or strategies for achieving them at each level (institutional and unit), assessment approaches and methodologies, sequence, and time frame. These may vary, based on the mission, goals, organization, and resources of the institu-

tion. Whatever the approach, effective assessment processes are useful, cost-effective, reasonably accurate and truthful, carefully planned, and organized, systematic, and sustained [p. 26].

Standards 7 (institutional assessment) and 14 (assessment of student learning) in *Characteristics of Excellence in Higher Education* are the major standards Middle States uses to determine institutional effectiveness:

Standard 7: "The institution has developed and implemented an assessment process that evaluates its overall effectiveness in achieving its mission and goals and its compliance with accreditation standards" (p. 25).

Standard 14: "Assessment of student learning demonstrates that, at graduation, or other appropriate points, the institution's students have knowledge, skills, and competencies consistent with institutional and appropriate higher education goals" (p. 63).

The two standards are similar, but standard 7 relates to institutional assessment as a whole, while standard 14 relates to student assessment in particular. Both standards are based on the cyclical process described in Chapters One and Two of this volume.

New England Association of Schools and Colleges, Commission on Institutions of Higher Education

In the preamble to its *Standards for Accreditation* (2005), the Commission on Institutions of Higher Education stresses the importance of the institutional effectiveness process:

Each of the eleven Standards articulates a dimension of institutional quality. In applying the Standards, the Commission assesses and makes a determination about the effectiveness of the institution as a whole. The institution that meets the Standards:

- Has clearly defined purposes appropriate to an institution of higher learning;
- Has assembled and organized those resources necessary to achieve its purposes;
- Is achieving its purposes; has the ability to continue to achieve its purposes [p. 1].

Institutional effectiveness is directly addressed by CIHE in standards 1 (Mission and Purpose) and 2 (Planning and Evaluation):

Standard 1, section 1.5: "The institution periodically re-evaluates the content and pertinence of its mission and purposes, assessing their usefulness in providing overall direction in planning and resource allocation. The results of this evaluation are used to enhance institutional effectiveness" (p. 3).

Standard 2, section 2.7: "The institution determines the effectiveness of its planning and evaluation activities on an ongoing basis. Results of these activities are used to further enhance the institution's implementation of its purposes and objectives" (p. 4).

Beyond these two standards, the term *institutional effectiveness* appears countless times in the Standards for Accreditation, as the organization stresses its importance in supporting academic programs, support services, governance, and virtually every other aspect of the institution. In fact, each of the eleven standards has its own section on institutional effectiveness.

North Central Association of Colleges and Schools, The Higher Learning Commission

In the North Central region, the Higher Learning Commission's *Handbook of Accreditation* (2003) has five criteria for accreditation. Criterion 2, Preparing for the Future, is concerned with institutional effectiveness: "The organization's allocation of resources and its processes for evaluation and planning demonstrate its capacity to fulfill its mission, improve the quality of its education, and respond to future challenges and opportunities" (p. 3.2.5). More specifically, core component 2C deals directly with institutional effectiveness: "The organization's ongoing evaluation and assessment processes provide reliable evidence of institutional effectiveness that clearly informs strategies for continuous improvement" (p. 3.2.7).

Interestingly, the commission provides "examples of evidence" that institutions can use to demonstrate their compliance with this criterion. These include evidence that an organization's performance matches its stated expectations; effective systems for collecting, analyzing, and using data; feedback loops used for continuous improvement; regular reviews of all academic and administrative units; and adequate support and resources for evaluation and assessment processes.

The Higher Learning Commission has also published the Commission Statement on Assessment of Student Learning, which is set out in the *Handbook of Accreditation* and is available on the commission's Web site. This statement provides a concise overview of the accountability movement in higher education:

> Among the public's many expectations of higher education, the most basic is that students will learn, and in particular that they will learn what they need to know to attain personal success and fulfill their public responsibilities in the twenty-first century. The focus has moved from considering resources as primary evidence of the quality of education to expecting documentation of student learning [Higher Learning Commission, 2003, p. 3.4.2].

NEW DIRECTIONS FOR COMMUNITY COLLEGES • DOI: 10.1002/cc

The statement goes on to stress that "faculty members should have the fundamental role in developing and sustaining systematic assessment of student learning" and concludes, "An organization committed to understanding and improving the learning opportunities and environments it provides students will be able to document the relationship between assessment of and improvement in student learning" (p. 3.4.2).

Northwest Commission on Colleges and Universities

Institutional effectiveness is an integral part of the mission statement of the Northwest Commission on Colleges and Universities:

> The mission of the Northwest Commission on Colleges and Universities (NWCCU) is to assure educational quality, enhance institutional effectiveness, and foster continuous improvement of colleges and universities in the Northwest region through analytical institutional self-assessment and critical peer review based upon evaluation criteria that are objectively and equitably applied to institutions with diverse missions, characteristics, and cultures [Northwest Commission on Colleges and Universities, 2003, p. 2].

Standard 1 of the nine standards in the NWCCU *Accreditation Handbook* (2003) is titled Institutional Mission and Goals, Planning and Effectiveness. Standard 1.A deals with Mission and Goals and standard 1.B with Planning and Effectiveness:

> The institution engages in ongoing planning to achieve its mission and goals. It also evaluates how well, and in what ways, it is accomplishing its mission and goals and uses the results for broad-based, continuous planning and evaluation. Through its planning process, the institution asks questions, seeks answers, analyzes itself, and revises its goals, policies, procedures, and resource allocation [p. 26].

Required documentation stated in the Accreditation Handbook includes the institution's mission statement, as well as details on outcomes:

> Evidence that demonstrates the analysis and appraisal of institutional outcomes. Examples may include:
> • Annual goals and assessment of success in their accomplishments;
> • Studies of alumni and former students;
> • Studies regarding effectiveness of programs and their graduates;
> • Studies that indicate degree of success in placing graduates;

- Pre- and post-test comparisons of student knowledge, skills, and abilities; and
- Surveys of satisfaction—students, alumni, and employees [p. 27].

Institutional effectiveness, though not often mentioned by name, is also part of other standards, including standard 2.B, Educational Program Planning and Assessment, and standard 5.E, Planning and Evaluation.

The NWCCU completed a revision of its *Standards for Accreditation* in January 2010, reducing the number of standards from nine to five. The fourth standard, Effectiveness and Improvement, is now directly related to institutional effectiveness. Most of the requirements and much of the language under standard 1.B have been moved to standard 4, which requires systematic data collection and analysis, defined procedures, and use of assessment results for program improvements. The standard reflects an expectation that assessment results are disseminated to the institution's constituencies. The standard has two subsections: 4.A, Assessment, and 4.B, Improvement. (Northwest Commission on Colleges and Universities, 2010).

Southern Association of Colleges and Schools Commission on Colleges

Institutional effectiveness is covered by name in two places in the *Principles of Accreditation* (2010). Core requirement 2.5 states, "The institution engages in ongoing, integrated, and institution-wide research-based planning and evaluation processes that (1) incorporate a systematic review of institutional mission, goals, and outcomes; (2) result in continuing improvement in institutional quality, and (3) demonstrate the institution is effectively accomplishing its mission" (p. 16), and comprehensive standard 3.3.1 states, "The institution identifies expected outcomes, assesses the extent to which it achieves these outcomes, and provides evidence of improvement based on analysis of the results in each of the following areas" (p. 25). The standard lists five specific program areas as separate substandards:

3.3.1.1   Educational programs, to include student learning outcomes
3.3.1.2   Administrative support services
3.3.1.3   Educational support services
3.3.1.4   Research within its educational mission, if appropriate
3.3.1.5   Community/public service within its educational mission, if appropriate [p. 25].

The difference between a core requirement and a comprehensive standard is that the former are basic, foundational standards that every institution must meet to become accredited, or to be continued in accreditation. Comprehensive standards are more specific to the operation of the institution, reflecting good practices in higher education that all member institutions are expected to meet.

Western Association of Schools and Accrediting Commission for Community and Junior Colleges

The Western Association of Schools and Colleges (WASC) has separate commissions for senior higher education institutions and community and junior colleges. The accreditation standards for the Accrediting Commission for Community Colleges and Junior Colleges (ACCJC) are set out in the *Accreditation Reference Handbook* (Accrediting Commission for Community and Junior Colleges, 2010). Reference Standard 1, Institutional Mission and Effectiveness, in the *Accreditation Reference Handbook* directly addresses institutional effectiveness:

> The institution demonstrates strong commitment to a mission that emphasizes achievement of student learning and to communicating the mission internally and externally. The institution uses analyses of quantitative and qualitative data and analysis in an ongoing and systematic cycle of evaluation, integrated planning, implementation, and re-evaluation to verify and improve the effectiveness by which the mission is accomplished [p. 15].

Part B of this standard, Improving Institutional Effectiveness, states, "The institution demonstrates its effectiveness by providing 1) evidence of the achievement of student learning outcomes and 2) evidence of institution and program performance. The institution uses ongoing and systematic evaluation and planning to refine its key processes and improve student learning" (p. 15). It then sets out seven requirements for all community colleges:

1. The institution maintains an ongoing, collegial, self-reflective dialogue about the continuous improvement of student learning and institutional processes.

2. The institution sets goals to improve its effectiveness consistent with its stated purposes. The institution articulates its goals and states the objectives derived from them in measurable terms so that the degree to which they are achieved can be determined and widely discussed. The institutional members understand these goals and work collaboratively toward their achievement.

3. The institution assesses progress toward achieving its stated goals and makes decisions regarding the improvement of institutional effectiveness in an ongoing and systematic cycle of evaluation, integrated planning, resource allocation, implementation, and reevaluation. Evaluation is based on analyses of both quantitative and qualitative data.

4. The institution provides evidence that the planning process is broad-based, offers opportunities for input by appropriate constituencies, allocates necessary resources, and leads to improvement of institutional effectiveness.

NEW DIRECTIONS FOR COMMUNITY COLLEGES • DOI: 10.1002/cc

5. The institution uses documented assessment results to communicate matters of quality assurance to appropriate constituencies.
6. The institution assures the effectiveness of its ongoing planning and resource allocation processes by systematically reviewing and modifying, as appropriate, all parts of the cycle, including institutional and other research efforts.
7. The institution assesses its evaluation mechanisms through a systematic review of their effectiveness in improving instructional programs, student support services, and library and other learning support services [pp. 15-16].

The commission has developed a "Rubric for Evaluating Institutional Effectiveness" that offers helpful guidance for an institution to do a self-evaluation of the quality of its institutional effectiveness activities (Accrediting Commission for Community and Junior Colleges, 2009). The rubric covers three characteristics of an institutional effectiveness program: program review, planning, and student learning outcomes. The institution can evaluate itself at one of four levels of proficiency: awareness, development, proficiency, or sustainable continuous quality improvement.

At WASC's senior college Web site, discussions of the nature, types, and uses of evidence in the *Evidence Guide* relate to assessing student learning outcomes (Accrediting Commission for Senior Colleges and Universities, 2002). This document discusses what constitutes good evidence and should be of great interest to all institutional effectiveness practitioners. Principles of "good" evidence are included, as well as things to avoid.

A Closer Look at Institutional Effectiveness in the SACSCOC Region

To provide a more detailed picture of the relationship between institutional effectiveness and accreditation, this section provides a case study of SACSCOC.

The role of institutional effectiveness in the SACSCOC accreditation process is best captured in the subtitle of the *Principles of Accreditation* (2009): *Foundations for Quality Enhancement*. Although two standards, core requirement 2.5 and comprehensive standard 3.3.1, are actually titled "institutional effectiveness," it is fair to say that the concept of institutional effectiveness permeates the entire accreditation process. Near the beginning of the *Principles* are these words:

At the heart of the Commission's philosophy of accreditation, the concept of quality enhancement presumes each member institution to be engaged in an ongoing program of improvement and be able to demonstrate how well it fulfills its stated mission. Although evaluation of an institution's educational quality and its effectiveness in achieving its mission is a difficult task requiring careful analysis and professional judgment, an institution is expected to document the quality and effectiveness of all its programs and services [p. 2].

In this section, we explore a few of the standards within the *Principles* and show how the concept of institutional effectiveness is the keystone of the accreditation process. We look specifically at core requirement 2.10 on student support services, comprehensive standard 3.8.2 on instruction in library use, and comprehensive standard 3.3.1.1 on institutional effectiveness in educational programs. Our premise is that virtually every accreditation standard can be viewed as a good-practice statement, as well as an institutional effectiveness standard. Applying a common methodology to each standard, we will find that the institution can improve its practices and its ability to maintain accreditation. The process should be transferable to other types of accreditation, not just regional accreditation by SACSCOC.

The basic process is as follows:

1. View the standard as a good-practice statement.
2. Conduct an internal audit of practices.
3. Build the audit process into the institution's institutional effectiveness process.
4. Reflect on the nonaccreditation benefits of the activity.

Case Study 1: Student Support Services.   Core requirement 2.10 of the *Principles of Accreditation* states: "The institution provides student support programs, services, and activities consistent with its mission that promote student learning and enhance the development of its students" (Southern Association of Colleges and Schools Commission on Colleges, 2010, p. 18). It is hard to argue against the underlying premises of this statement as representing sound practice. It is important that the institution act in ways consistent with its mission. And although student services can offer entertainment and convenience to students, making a difference in the lives of students has to matter. This standard thus sets out three good practices:

- Being mission driven within student support services
- Promotion of student learning through student support services
- Enhancement of the development of students through student support services

The first step in our internal audit is the easy one: make a list. What services, programs, and activities offerings does the institution offer? Then we ask, "How are we doing?" Do these practices match the good practices? Note that the good-practice statement (the standard) does not refer to any single office on campus, so the audit might need to cut across the organization chart. We will gather information on student academic support services such as tutoring, disability accommodations, and career and placement programs. We need to consider traditional student services such as judicial review, student government, intramurals, orientation, heath and wellness, and counseling. The college offers administrative services directly to students such as registrar functions, financial aid, and food services, and it tailors these services differently to distance education students or those at off-campus sites.

For the next step, which is the hard one, we ask three questions about each item on the list:

- Can we articulate how it is mission relevant?
- Can we articulate how student learning or student development is intended to occur?
- What evidence do we have that this student learning or development is actually taking place?

This examination will uncover that some services, such as parts of financial aid and registrar activities, might be mission related but not directly learning related; these are important, but more in an administrative sense. The examination will also discover that asking the three questions above can easily lead to answers of "no," "no," and "none," respectively. Would that be an uncomfortable finding? Probably, but note how helpful the exercise is. Also note how the good practice statement, when audited carefully, forces us to see that we cannot possibly move forward without incorporating the findings into an institutional effectiveness process.

We can research professional organizations to get an indication of what are considered good practices for student service provision. The following organizations might help with this information:

- Student Affairs Administrators in Higher Education
- American College Counseling Association
- American Association of Collegiate Registrars and Admissions Officers
- National Academic Advising Association
- National Orientation Directors Association

Institutional effectiveness within the *Principles of Accreditation* (and this is not unique to SACSCOC) centers around a three-phase process: developing expected outcomes, assessing actual versus expected results, and using the results of the process to make improvements. Consider how the audit exercise gets translated into the institutional effectiveness process for the case of tutoring services for students. We have to start with the end in mind: determining our expected outcomes—for example, better grades in developmental or gatekeeper classes, better student persistence, student satisfaction with the services, or coverage of services to the most critical

NEW DIRECTIONS FOR COMMUNITY COLLEGES • DOI: 10.1002/cc

classes. How will we know success when we see it? Who will do the measuring? Can we obtain counts or logs by class and section? Are satisfaction surveys already in use? Can we use our student information system to determine the performance of students using the services versus other similar students? Are we collecting actionable data—information that will let us know where our strengths and weaknesses lie so that we can enhance our strengths and address our weaknesses?

Suppose we find that students who took advantage of English tutoring did better (measured by, for example, retention, grades in the current class, or grades in the next class) than those who did not, but math-tutored students showed no difference. Also, thirty students said on their satisfaction surveys that they wish tutors were available for economics. We dig deeper and consider the options: a different approach in math or an enhanced training program for student tutors? Closer coordination of exam schedules and tutoring schedules? Initiate tutoring in economics? Replace math tutoring with economics tutors? Better publicity for English tutoring?

By starting with a simple good-practices statement, we are now equipped through the institutional effectiveness system to reap important benefits unrelated to simply showing compliance with an accreditation standard. We can deal with such issues as streamlining activities to match the institutional mission by cutting inappropriate programs and expanding those that can most help students. We become data driven in this process and can articulate student service needs to foundations and other potential benefactors. All of this can arise from an accreditation standard that does not appear on the surface to relate to institutional effectiveness. Another benefit is a dynamite narrative in the materials we might need to send to our regional accreditor.

Case Study 2: Instruction in Library Use.   Comprehensive standard 3.8.2 of the *Principles of Accreditation* states, "The institution ensures that users have access to regular and timely instruction in the use of the library and other learning/information resources" (p. 29). Again, it is hard to quibble with this as a good-practice statement. Interpreting the standard leads to these practices:

- Instruction in the use of the physical library facility
- Instruction in the use of virtual library facilities
- Access to bibliographical instruction
- Access to computer lab instruction
- Timely and regular programming
- Access for all users: day and night; traditional and online students; on the main campus and off-campus sites; and for students, faculty, and staff

For the internal audit, a list is a good place to start. But where do we get the information? Clearly the library and information technology (IT) staffs are logical starting places, but activity might be decentralized. Perhaps a survey of faculty to see what activities they originate would be appropriate. But is the instruction timely, and how would we know? This could mean a survey of users or potential users of the instruction, as well as a look at external bodies that might have expertise in this area. Good starting places are groups like EDUCAUSE and the Association of College and Research Libraries. Data on attendance at training sections could be compiled, and attendees could be classified by type of student or faculty or staff member. We could ask if the instruction is voluntary or mandatory. If voluntary, we could try to find out the percentage of coverage of the target population. In all cases we could determine who is responsible for ensuring delivery.

The very nature of the questions asked in the audit phase points to the importance of embedding this good practice statement into the institution's institutional effectiveness process. Surely the institution is interested in more than the number and frequency of programs offered; the quality of the programming is critical. This means that expected outcomes might include learning outcomes for students and other users and evidence of increased use of library and learning resources.

Consider the delivery of instruction in the use of the physical library and bibliographical instruction. Desirable outcomes include the ability of students to:

- Use the stacks, reference room, and print periodicals successfully
- Conduct effective searches using online databases
- Understand the difference between credible and other sources when using the Internet
- Cite sources correctly

Within the institutional effectiveness process, these outcomes could be set forth in measurable terms, and clear responsibility for program delivery and assessment can be determined.

The benefits of embedding the accreditation standard into the institutional effectiveness process are clear. Programs should become better targeted to the needs of users. Coordination of activities among library staff, IT staff, and faculty could be enhanced. Unnecessary duplication of activities can be lessened. Note that many of the benefits of treating the standard as a good-practice statement may be only loosely related to the goal of meeting accreditation requirements.

Case Study 3: Institutional Effectiveness in Educational Programs. The most commonly cited standard for noncompliance within the SACSCOC membership is the standard on institutional effectiveness itself, comprehensive standard 3.3.1. For community colleges undergoing reaffirmation in 2010, 70 percent of these institutions were found out of compliance with this standard during the initial (off-site) phase of review, and 30 percent of these received a recommendation on this standard in their official reports following on-site review. After submitting a response to the recommendation and after SACSCOC review of their reaffirmation materials, 20 percent of these institutions were required to file a monitoring report on this standard. The data clearly show that the most common issue is institutional effectiveness activity within educational programs. The standard and its subpart read as follows:

3.3.1 The institution identifies expected outcomes, assesses the extent to which it achieves these outcomes, and provides evidence of improvement based on analysis of the results in each of the following areas: (Institutional Effectiveness)
   3.3.1.1 educational programs, to include student learning outcomes [p. 25].

More than any other aspect of accreditation, institutional effectiveness is an area that can benefit from viewing the standard as a statement of good practice rather than just an accrediting requirement. The standard calls for institutions to be systematic in trying to make programs better—programs that are already strong as well as those that are weak. The standard suggests looking at both process and learning goals. The emphasis, however, is on what happens to student learning—the most important output of the educational process.

An internal audit in this case is often a bit more difficult than in the other standards discussed previously. In some cases, the goals of the program are relatively clear; technical programs and professional education are much easier to assess than are more traditional liberal arts disciplines because often a professional license or examination is needed to practice in the field. But there is benefit in simply sitting down and asking, "What are the outcomes that really matter in our discipline—both expected program outcomes and program student learning outcomes?" Not all of these will be in measurable terms, but it is a good place to start. Another question must also be asked: How will we know success when we see it? Can we start to develop measures, even proxy measures, of the desired outcomes? Only after we do this process can we look for evidence of success. Too many times, the institutional effectiveness process for educational programs starts with the measures and works to the outcomes (for example, "We are going to give the Collegiate Assessment of Academic Proficiency exam or administer the Community College Survey of Student Engagement. What are our expected outcomes?"); not only is this putting the proverbial cart before the horse, it is intellectually dishonest.

The next step in the internal audit process is to turn toward evidence of meeting expected outcomes. Do we have any useful measures? Do we have, or can we get, actionable data that will allow us to pinpoint where the program's strengths and weaknesses are? The most important element of this process in an academic setting is that it be a program-level exercise. Improvement of an educational program requires the faculty in the same discipline to enter into a conversation as to what is expected of a graduate.

Again, turning to respected external groups can help:

- North Carolina State University's Internet Resources for Higher Education Outcomes Assessment
- Discipline-specific materials such as those by specialty accreditors like the Accreditation Board for Engineering and Technology or discipline-specific professional organizations such as the American Psychological Association's The Assessment Cyberguide for Learning Goals and Outcomes (2009) or the National Communication Association
- The Association for Institutional Research and the Southern Association for Institutional Research for multiple resources on improving assessment in educational programs

The contribution of the institutional effectiveness process is to give structure to the discussion of program improvement. The flow from expected outcomes, to assessment, to use of results for improvement must be emphasized. Institutional effectiveness is based on this axiom: "Start with the end in mind." Institutional effectiveness tends to fail when the emphasis is placed elsewhere—for example, starting with a particular assessment instrument in mind.

The other key failure is being satisfied with assessments that yield no actionable data. This occurs because faculty members become convinced the institutional effectiveness system is for someone else, not for them. The goal becomes reporting results on something to make the administration or a regional body go away. In such a case, the real institutional effectiveness system takes place somewhere else, as faculty make program improvements in a nonsystematic, unreported way. Only if the process is viewed as something beneficial to the faculty at the program level will a community college have any chance of developing an effective institutional effectiveness system. When the faculty get on board, the benefits are large and lasting. There will be more systematic thinking about educational goals, a means to celebrate success as well as improve weaknesses, and, most important, something that will keep the institution true to its mission to enhance the lives of its students.

Conclusion

Community and technical colleges that treat regional accreditation standards (or any other set of accrediting standards) as a series of good-practice statements and institutionalize them into the operations of the institution will reap clear benefits. Conducting internal audits of performance relative to these good practices naturally leads to their inclusion into the institutional effectiveness process, which is one of those good practices.

An institutional effectiveness system that exists because the accreditor says "you have to do it" can be a terrible drag on a college. In this chapter, we have offered some examples that may help practitioners build an institutional mind-set that the reason for determining expected outcomes and assessing those outcomes is to give the institution the actionable data needed to move forward. If this is done, the benefits will become clear. As a bonus, perhaps one of these benefits will be a smoother and less stressful accreditation process.

References

Accrediting Commission for Community and Junior Colleges. Accreditation Reference Handbook. Novato, Calif.: Accrediting Commission for Community and Junior Colleges, August 2010. Retrieved February 11, 2011, from http://www.accjc.org/wp-content/uploads/2010/09/Accreditation-Reference-Handbook-August-20101.pdf.

Accrediting Commission for Community and Junior Colleges. Rubric for Evaluating Institutional Effectiveness. Novato, Calif.: Accrediting Commission for Community and Junior Colleges, 2009. Retrieved February 11, 2011, from http://www.accjc.org/wp-content/uploads/2010/09/Rubric%20for%20Evaluating%20Institutional%20Effectiveness.pdf.

Accrediting Commission for Senior Colleges and Universities. Evidence Guide: A Guide to Using Evidence in the Accreditation Process. Novato, Calif.: Accrediting Commission for Senior Colleges and Universities Western Association of Schools and Colleges, 2002. Retrieved February 11, 2011, from http://www.wascsenior.org/findit/files/forms/EvidenceGuide_Jan_02.pdf.

American Psychological Association. The Assessment CyberGuide for Learning Goals and Outcomes (2nd ed., November 2009), Compiled by Thomas Pusateri. Retrieved February 11, 2011, from http://www.apa.org/ed/governance/bea/assessment-cyberguide-v2.pdf.

Commission on Institutions of Higher Education. Standards for Accreditation. Bedford, Mass.: Commission on Institutions of Higher Education, 2006. Retrieved March 3, 2011, from http://cihe.neasc.org/downloads/Standards/Standards_for_Accreditation__2006.pdf.

The Higher Learning Commission. Commission Statement on Assessment of Student Learning. Chicago: The Higher Learning Commission, February 2003. Retrieved on February 11. 2011, from http://content.springcm.com/content/Download Documents.ashx?Selection=Document%2C20177502%3B&accountId=5968.

The Higher Learning Commission. Handbook of Accreditation. (3rd ed.) Chicago: The Higher Learning Commission, 2003. Retrieved February 11, 2011, from http://content.springcm.com/content/DownloadDocuments.ashx?Selection=Document%2C 10611003%3B&accountId=5968.

Middle States Commission on Higher Education. Characteristics of Excellence in Higher Education. (12th ed.) Philadelphia: Middle States Commission on Higher Education, 2009. Retrieved February 11, 2011, from http://www.msche.org/publications/CHX06_Aug08REVMarch09.pdf.

New England Association for Schools and Colleges. Standards for Accreditation. Retrieved February 11, 2011 from http://cpss.neasc.org/getting_started/standards_for_accreditation/.

Northwest Commission on Colleges and Universities. Accreditation Handbook. (2003 ed.). Redmond, Wash.: Northwest Commission on Colleges and Universities, updated

June 23, 2008. Retrieved February 11, 2011, from http://www.nwccu.org/Pubs%20 Forms%20and%20Updates/Publications/Accreditation%20Handbook.pdf.

Northwest Commission on Colleges and Universities. NWCCU Standards of Accreditation. Redmond, Wash.: Northwest Commission on Colleges and Universities, 2010. Retrieved February 11, 2011, from http://www.nwccu.org/Pubs%20Forms%20 and%20Updates/Publications/Standards%20for%20Accreditation.pdf.

Southern Association of Colleges and Schools Commission on Colleges. Principles of Accreditation: Foundations for Quality Enhancement. (2010 ed.) Decatur, Ga.: Southern Association of Colleges and Schools Commission on Colleges, 2010. Retrieved February 11, 2011, from http://www.sacscoc.org/pdf/2010Principlesof Accreditation.pdf.

RONALD B. HEAD *serves as a special projects officer at Tidewater Community College in Norfolk, Virginia; teaches doctoral education courses online for the University of Phoenix; and does consulting work in accreditation and institutional effectiveness.*

MICHAEL S. JOHNSON *is a vice president at the Southern Association of Colleges and Schools Commission on Colleges.*

NEW DIRECTIONS FOR COMMUNITY COLLEGES • DOI: 10.1002/cc

5

The office of institutional research (IR) at a community college can provide valuable assistance in supporting accreditation and institutional effectiveness using this proven model.

The Community College IR Shop and Accreditation: A Case Study

George Johnston

The following community colleges were examined in the study presented in this chapter: Diablo Valley College (California), Greenfield Community College (Massachusetts), Johnson County Community College (Kansas), LaGuardia Community College (New York), Parkland College (Illinois), Santa Fe College (Florida), Shelton State Community College (Alabama), St. Louis Community College (Missouri), Tidewater Community College (Virginia), and Wenatchee Valley College (Washington). Jeffrey Seybert, director of the College Benchmarking Project, and Fred Lillbridge, institutional research director at Dona Ana Community College, New Mexico, and past president of the Association for Institutional Research, were interviewed by phone and e-mail.

This chapter presents results of a study I recently conducted on the role of traditional institutional research (IR) offices in support of accreditation activities and institutional effectiveness. The purpose of the study was to confirm or disconfirm the utility of a theoretical model developed by Brittingham, O'Brien, and Alig (2008) of the role of IR offices in the accreditation process, based on a case study of two-year comprehensive community colleges across the country. Community colleges for the study were selected to capture possible variations based on size and location, including state and regional accrediting agency. All six regional accrediting agencies were represented in the sample, and no more than one institution from a state was included.

NEW DIRECTIONS FOR COMMUNITY COLLEGES, no. 153, Spring 2011 © 2011 Wiley Periodicals, Inc.
Published online in Wiley Online Library (wileyonlinelibrary.com) • DOI: 10.1002/cc.436

Little research has been done on the role of IR offices with respect to the accreditation process, particularly for two-year, comprehensive community colleges, and Brittingham, O'Brien, and Alig's model is promising in this respect. Traditionally, the IR office has played three key roles in providing the support necessary to transform data into information: custodian or keeper of the data, broker of the process of transferring the data into information, and manager or processor of the information and application to a situation (McLaughlin, Howard, Balkan, and Blythe, 1998). Increasingly, however, external forces are shaping the functions of institutional research, and one of the major forces has been accreditation (Morest and Jenkins, 2007).

Recent research on the role of IR in accreditation includes work by Christensen (2007), Morest and Jenkins (2007), and Brittingham, O'Brien, and Alig (2008). Brittingham, O'Brien, and Alig's study presented a model that set out both traditional and possible new roles that IR offices might consider for the future. While the model appears to be designed primarily for four-year institutions, it seems applicable to two-year comprehensive community colleges as well.

The theoretical model that Brittingham, O'Brien, and Alig proposed served as a basis for looking more deeply at the role of the IT office in the regional accreditation process. The authors proposed that both traditional and emerging roles were possible; my study examined each of these roles and compared them with responses by directors of institutional research and self-study coordinators at the colleges sampled.

Traditional Roles for IR Offices

The office of Institutional Research (IR) is often called upon to assist in the accreditation and institutional effectiveness process. Some of these roles are traditional at least for community colleges that have had IR shops for some time.

Serve on Self-Study Steering Committee. All of the respondents reported that although the actual organization of the self-study team varied, one or more representatives from the institutional research office played key roles in working with the group responsible for completing the self-study document. As Brittingham, O'Brien, and Alig (2008) noted, "The institutional researcher understands that data are meant to 'tell a story' about the institution and can assist the self-study's writers in deciding which data are the most effective means through which to tell a particular story and how the data can be most effectively displayed" (p. 70).

Take Responsibility for Getting the Data Forms Complete. Some regional accreditors have specific data forms that must be completed. For example, the Southern Association of Colleges and Schools Commission on Colleges (2009) reaffirms institutions every ten years but requires an elaborate interim report during the fifth year between reaffirmations. Santa Fe Community College was one of the pilot colleges to test the newly revised standards of the Fifth-Year Interim Report, which for the first time included an abbreviated compliance certification. Tidewater Community College also provided leadership in the development of electronic transmission of data forms to the Southern Association of Colleges (Head and Kleiman, 2006). Tidewater reported that all of the data submitted for the compliance aspect of the new self-study was done by the IR office. LaGuardia Community College reported that its IR office is responsible for completing all Middle States Association of Colleges and Schools data forms and surveys. The Higher Learning Commission (HLC) does not require specific data forms unless an institution is under some form of monitoring, but it does require data to be reported within the self-study itself or the biennial portfolio used in the Academic Quality Improvement Program (AQIP). Johnson County Community College was one of the first colleges to implement the AQIP model. The Northwest Commission on Colleges and Universities is modifying its requirements to include biennial reports within a seven-year cycle, with two campus visits during the full cycle (Baker, 2009). Wenatchee Valley College was one of four pilot institutions involved in the new process.

Supply Self-Study Teams with Additional Data, Useful Institutional Data, and Reports.   Brittingham, O'Brien, and Alig (2008) note that "every institution has more data than it uses" (p. 70). The data that they are referring to include fact books, annual reports, survey results, and strategic planning documents. Many of the data that the various self-study committees use are often stored and maintained by IR offices. Sometimes these data are referred to as dashboard indicators or indicators of institutional effectiveness (Seybert, 2007; Johnston and Kristovich, 2000) or, more commonly, as benchmarks (Seybert, 2003; Alfred, Shults, and Seybert, 2007). Some states, including Florida, Virginia, Indiana, and New Hampshire, collect these data at the state level (Toutkoushian and Massa, 2008).

A number of responders reported that they regularly administered various externally created surveys, including the Community College Survey of Student Engagement (CCSSE), and the Noel-Levitz College Student Inventory CCSSE, established in 2001, provides information on student engagement as a key indicator (indirect) of student learning and offers nationally recognized benchmarks in key areas. Colleges can also add questions designed specifically for their own institutions. In 2009, 324 colleges were listed as participants, although not all of these were independent institutions. Noel-Levitz is a privately owned for-profit group established in 1984 and claims more than two thousand collaborations with colleges and universities. It does surveys for admissions management, financial aid, marketing, and retention. Both instruments are expensive, and consequently many community colleges do not administer them every year.

Another source of data available to institutional researchers is the National Community College Benchmarking Project, housed at Johnson County Community College in Kansas (Seybert, 2003). This project, piloted in 2003, sets out twenty-five benchmarks that can be used for comparison purposes. The value of benchmarking lies in providing the means by which institutions can identify best practices that peer institutions use (Sheldon and Durdella, 2006). In 2008, 185 community colleges participated in the project, including several from this case study.

Diablo Valley College reported it used an ACT instrument, the Student Opinion Survey, on a two-year cycle. Institutional research respondents expressed serious concern about the extent to which they might be able to use such instruments in the future as budgets become increasingly tight. Tidewater used the ACT Student Opinion Survey for a number of years but has eliminated its use.

Identify and Obtain Additional Data.   The Brittingham, O'Brien, and Alig (2008) model suggests that IR offices may be uniquely positioned to quickly develop any additional data that may be required through additional surveys or other data collection methods. It is often preferable to have one source within the college, rather than individual committees, develop surveys. Several respondents noted that their IR office served as a central clearinghouse for any new campus survey instruments. This can create some tensions when faculty members feel that their prerogatives of academic freedom are compromised by IR offices that are acting as a central clearinghouse for all surveys on campus. There is also a clear danger of survey fatigue for both students and faculty. In addition, legal questions are associated with research using human subjects.

Depending on the size of its office, IR may (or may not) have the expertise necessary to help assist in developing qualitative and quantitative research instruments. Morest and Jenkins (2007) report that more than half of the IR offices have one or fewer full-time research professionals. With limited or no IR staff, some studies deemed desirable might not be conducted, reducing data available to inform decision making, including the self-study. If IR staff members lack experience in social science research, they might not ask important questions or interpret the answers insightfully, even if the validity of the data is not at issue.

What seems to be fairly common among the respondents is that in addition to developing data reports for internal use, as well as for regular federal, state, and regional accrediting agencies, a certain amount of institutional time and energy must be committed to meeting the needs of the specialized accrediting agencies for disciplinary programs within the colleges. The net result is that IR offices spend significant time and energy on meeting all of the compliance requirements, raising the question of the hidden costs for compliance.

Set Up an Intranet Site for Exhibits and Catalogue What Is Available.   For traditional self-study site visits, it is not uncommon for a room to be set aside at the college that will have all of the resources the visiting team needs to gain a complete picture of the college. One of the impacts of the computer age is that these materials and others are increasingly available electronically, or what Nate Dickmeyer of LaGuardia Community College refers to as digital storytelling. Some respondents reported that their college has completed the move to intranet sites, while others are seemingly even more transparent by posting their self-study on the Internet, thereby making it available to all stakeholders, not just in-house intranet users. Diablo Valley Community College's full self-study is available online at http://www.dvc.edu/org/info/accreditation/pdfs/DVCAccreditatonSelfStudy07-08.pdf. And St. Louis Community College has its most recent self-study online at www.stlcc.edu/About/NCA_HLC_Self_Study/SelfStudy_Results.html. Johnson County Community College has a copy of its most recent AQIP Portfolio Assessment online at www.jccc.edu/home/download/16331/AQIPPortfolio.pdf. AQIP portfolios tend to be much shorter (under one hundred pages) than the typical self-study and are reviewed by an external off-site panel every two years. Links to all AQIP institution's system portfolios can be found on the HLC Web site (http://www.hlcommission.org/aqip-systems-appraisal/systems-portfolios-links.html).

One of the challenges in using electronic media is how to store and present assessment of student learning data in a context that makes sense and is useful. Parkland College has an Internet site dedicated to program assessment (http://www2.parkland.edu/accreditation.html). The Diablo Valley College Web site has links to more complete data on student learning outcomes (www.dvc.edu/org/departments/research/slo/index.htm).

New Roles for IR Offices

In addition to traditional roles, IR shops have the opportunity to expand the ways in which they provide assistance to community colleges during the accreditation process.

Help the Self-Study Team Understand the Data Now Available. Brittingham, O'Brien, and Alig's (2008) model suggests that IR offices can be of significant service to the institution, especially when there has been a history of limited understanding of data and its uses. Several institutions reported that their senior administrators were not always familiar or comfortable using data to help make decisions. In such situations, IR offices can be particularly helpful in understanding trend data. Susan Murray from Wenatchee Community College noted that there are increasing expectations for analysis and synthesis of data by regional accrediting bodies. Community college faculty and staff who have not spent a lot of time thinking about trend data sometimes need coaching. This function often falls on the IR office, particularly as college budgets are becoming leaner.

Help the Institution Define Success. It is possible that of all the aspects of the model under consideration, this role may prove the most useful and important. The model has three separate steps closely related to the concept of understanding success:

1. Define success for the institution.
2. Help the institution learn the value of negative findings.
3. Help the institution make progress on assessment of student learning.

Brittingham, O'Brien, and Alig (2008) note that "the key to establishing a culture of inquiry is willingness to accept `negative results' and use them as the basis for developing realistic plans to address identified weaknesses" (p. 73). Because of the apparent similarity of these two roles, I have combined them into a single step: defining success.

An approach to the overall assessment process that seems to be increasingly common includes variations on models for continuous improvement. For example, Shelton State Community College has developed an ongoing quality improvement process it calls TEAMSpirit, modeled on the continuous improvement model of the Malcolm Baldrige National Quality Award, and participates in the Alabama Quality Award. Although Shelton State is accredited by SACS, one of the links on its quality improvement page is the HLC AQIP home page. Johnson County Community College also participates in the statewide quality improvement system for Kansas, as does St. Louis Community College with a similar system in Missouri.

Until recently, it was uncommon for a relatively healthy community college to receive anything but a ten-year renewal of accreditation. Recent changes in accreditation can be traced to the report to Secretary of Education Margaret Spellings on the future of higher education (Secretary of Education's Commission on the Future, 2006): regional accrediting bodies are now requiring shorter cycles between visits (from ten down to seven years), as well as a greater emphasis on objectively defined data. One consequence can be the perception that an institution that is reaffirmed only every seven or ten years is somehow underperforming based on previous expectations.

The IR office can serve a helpful function by helping the self-study team be more realistic in its expectations for accreditation periods. Regional bodies are also becoming more demanding. Diablo Valley College, which prides itself on being one of the premier California community colleges based on its large numbers of transfers to the University of California at Berkeley and other prestigious four-year institutions, recently found itself in danger of accreditation sanctions because of a lack of progress in evaluating student learning outcomes. There is very little an IR office can do to sugarcoat such findings except, perhaps, to help the institution develop a new response to the changed environment.

Closing the Loop.   As Brittingham, O'Brien, and Alig (2008) note, much of the accreditation process involves "closing the loop" (p. 74), which posits three closely related roles that can be combined into a single response:

- Reading the report
- Reading the action letter and planning for the next report
- Helping to determine which data to disclose to the public

All respondents reported that they had been involved in the reading and evaluating of the self-study report. In many cases they served on the final editing committee.

The process of closing the loop can mean many different things. In a continuous improvement model that many of the colleges are moving toward or have fully embraced, closing the loop can be traced back at least as far as Nichols (1995). Nichols proposed a five-stage model that flows from the college's mission and purposes statements, to its goals (academic outcomes), to clearly identified assessment methods and criteria, to the collection of results, to the use of those results to create changes that cause the cycle to begin all over again.

Nathan Dickmeyer (personal correspondence, June 2009) reported that in response to the Middle States Association of Colleges and Schools requirement for more measurable outcomes, the IR office at LaGuardia Community College has developed a checklist for committees charged with formulating recommendations. He notes that "too many committees have simply put down their favorite ideas after many meetings with no supporting evidence as to the size or intensity of the problem or the probable success of the recommendation."

Several of the respondents who asked not to be identified said that closing the loop was perhaps the most difficult and frustrating part of the accreditation process. They told stories of identifying obvious instances where the loop had not been closed, only to encounter significant pushback by faculty and staff. There can be serious consequences to the institution if loopholes that the site visit team finds are not addressed. Some faculty and staff seem to believe that regional bodies are not serious in requiring evidence of compliance. There is a need to reinforce the notion that a new normal is in place.

In terms of helping to determine which data to report to the public, most of the respondents pointed to the Internet Web sites that were available to the general public. As Nathan Dickmeyer said, "I have no idea why anything should be withheld."

The Costs Associated with Accountability

The model that Brittingham, O'Brien, and Alig (2008) created appears to fairly accurately describe many of the roles that IR offices play in the regional accreditation process, with the possible exception that changes may soon occur on even shorter cycles than the authors anticipated, and electronic sharing of the results to a broad array of stakeholders through the Internet seems increasingly likely. Given the fact that IR offices in most cases also provide the data and analysis for federal and state agencies, as well as other specialized accrediting bodies, one can only wonder at what point their staffs become stretched beyond reasonable limits, leaving little time for other research needed to answer institutional questions.

As Morest and Jenkins (2007) noted in their research findings, many IR offices spend a great deal of time satisfying compliance requirements. Although many of the data compiled and analyzed by the typical IR office are needed and used for accreditation, such data may be of limited use to the institutions in learning about students or in program improvement. Morest and Jenkins argue that such compliance reporting is so time-consuming that it may take away from other more useful research, such as a careful examination of remedial students and the best practices for helping them advance. Nevertheless, they note that such compliance reporting is nonnegotiable. It might be informative at some point to consider the full cost associated with accountability.

Conclusion

Several additional suggestions came up during the interviews. It was quite obvious that support from the president was considered critical for the IR office. Not all presidents know how to take full advantage of the possibilities that exist in a fully functioning IR office, however. It is likely that under new and emerging accreditation requirements that emphasize continuous improvement and clearly defined results, presidents and chief academic officers will need to rely more and more on their IR office.

A second suggestion was that one or more persons in the IR office, or at least one or more members on the self-study team, should be trained as a peer reviewer in their regional association. More than half of the respondents reported that they either were or had been peer reviewers.

A third suggestion was that wherever possible, staff in the IR office should become active in their state and national IR associations, including the Association for Institutional Research (the national organization for two- and four-year institutions), the National Community College Council for Research and Planning (a council affiliated with the American Association for Community Colleges), and even the Council for the Study of Community Colleges (a council affiliated with American Association for Community Colleges for individuals involved in research about the community colleges).

References

Alfred, R., Shults, C., and Seybert, J. A. *Core Indicators of Effectiveness for Community Colleges.* Washington, D.C.: American Association of Community Colleges, 2007.
Baker, R. L. "Overview of the Revised Accreditation Standards and New Oversight Process." Presentation at the annual meeting of the Northwest Commission of Colleges and Universities, 2009. Retrieved from http://www.nwccu.org/Revised%20Standards%20Workshop/StandardsWorkshop.htm on February 1, 2011.
Brittingham, B., O'Brien, P. M., and Alig, J. L. "Accreditation and Institutional Research: The Traditional Role and New Dimensions." Institutional Research: More Than Just Research. Dawn Geronimo Terkla. (ed.) New Directions for Higher Education, no. 141. San Francisco: Jossey-Bass, 2008. (EJ 791 433)
Christensen, G. "The Role of Institutional Researcher in Accreditation: The Indispensable Researcher." Paper presented at the annual meeting of Association for Institutional Research in Upper Midwest. Bloomington, MN. Oct. 26–27, 2007.

Head, R., and Kleiman, L. "Compliance Certification in the Electronic Age: A Case Study from Tidewater Community College." Presentation at the annual meeting of the Southern Association of Colleges and Schools, Orlando, Fla., Dec. 6, 2006.

Johnston, G. H., and Kristovich, S. A. R. "Community College Alchemists: Turning Data into Information." Dimensions of Managing Academic Affairs in the Community College. Douglas Robiallard, Jr. (ed.) New Directions for Community Colleges, no. 109. San Francisco: Jossey-Bass, Spring, 2000. (EJ 605410).

McGuire, P. A. "Accreditation's Benefits for Individuals and Institutions." Accreditation: Assuring and Enhancing Quality. Patricia M. O'Brian. (ed.) New Directions for Higher Education, no. 145. San Francisco: Jossey-Bass, 2009. (EJ 833646).

McLaughlin, G. W., Howard, R. D., Balkan, L. A., and Blythe, E. W. *People, Processes, and Managing Data*. Tallahassee, Fla.: Association for Institutional Research, 1998.

Morest, V. A. and Jenkins, D. "Institutional Research and the Culture of Evidence at Community Colleges," Achieving the Dream: Community Colleges Count. New York: Community College Research Center (Teachers College Columbia University). 2007.

Nichols, J. O. *A Practitioner's Handbook for Institutional Effectiveness and Student Outcomes Assessment Implementation*. (3rd ed.) New York: Agathon Press, 1995.

Seybert, J. A. "Spotlight on Community Colleges: Benchmarking Project Gains Momentum." Business Officers, 40, National Association of College and University Business Officers, 2007.

Seybert, J. A. "Benchmarking Community College Instructional Costs and Productivity: The Kansas Study" Paper presented at the 108th Annual meeting of the Higher Learning Commission of the North Central Association of Colleges and Schools. Chicago, IL. April 13–16, 2003.

Sheldon, C. Q., and Durdella, N. R. "Key Resources on Benchmarking in Community Colleges." Benchmarking: an essential tool for assessment, improvement, and accountability. Stella M. Flores (ed.) New Directions for Community Colleges, no. 134. San Francisco: Jossey-Bass, 2006.

Southern Association of Colleges and Schools Commission on Colleges. *Principles of Accreditation: Foundations for Quality Enhancement* (2010 ed.). Decatur, Ga.: Southern Association of Colleges and Schools Commission on Colleges, 2009. Retrieved from http://www.sacscoc.org/pdf/2010PrinciplesofAccreditation.pdf on February 1, 2011.

Toutkoushian, R. K., and Massa, T. R. "Editor's Notes". Robert K. Toutkoushian and Tod R. Massa (eds.) Conducting Institutional Research in Non-Campus-Based Settings. New Directions for Institutional Research, no. 139. San Francisco: Jossey-Bass, 2008.

GEORGE JOHNSTON recently retired from Parkland College in Champaign, Illinois, where he served as director of the Office of Institutional Research for several years.

NEW DIRECTIONS FOR COMMUNITY COLLEGES • DOI: 10.1002/cc

Program reviews have multiple purposes and designs. While focused on units within the college, the compilation of reviews also provides evidence of institutional effectiveness.

Program Review and Institutional Effectiveness

Trudy Bers

The purpose of this chapter is to identify key ways in which program review provides information and documentation demonstrating that a community college is effective. This is accomplished through both the program review process (the means by which reviews are conducted) and the product (program review reports and supporting evidence). The various purposes of program review are discussed in the context of how they support institutional effectiveness. Several program review models are described: a standardized model, a free-form model, a model based on external evaluation and self-studies, outside expert reviews, and a mixed model. Similarities and differences in reviews for instructional and noninstructional departments are observed. The chapter concludes with a discussion of guiding principles for program reviews and the linkage with institutional effectiveness.

Two key definitions shape this chapter. The first is a definition of *institutional effectiveness*, which I view as an ongoing, integrated, and systematic set of institutional processes that a college uses to determine and ensure the quality of its academic and support programs and administrative functions. The process includes planning, evaluating programs and services, identifying and measuring learning outcomes, and using data and assessment results for making decisions that result in improved programs, services, and institutional quality. The second definition is that of program review: a type of evaluation of an instructional, instructional support, student service, or

New Directions for Community Colleges, no. 153, Spring 2011 © 2011 Wiley Periodicals, Inc.
Published online in Wiley Online Library (wileyonlinelibrary.com) • DOI: 10.1002/cc.437

administrative program, department, or unit. Note that this definition covers virtually all departments within an institution, not just instructional programs. As well, note that I use the terms *program, department,* and *unit* interchangeably.

Institutional effectiveness is a broad umbrella concept, and program review is a specific activity that enables an instructional or administrative unit to evaluate its effectiveness on a number of dimensions. Institutional research (IR) offices are important contributors to both institutional effectiveness and program review. Often the institutional effectiveness or program review function, or both, is overseen by the IR office, but even if not, IR provides accurate, timely, and uniform data based on clear and uniform operational definitions.

Although the focus of program review is on a unit, reviews, taken together, provide information and documentation demonstrating whether a community college is effective or not. Program review forces the institution to look at its parts, though I note that the overall nature, culture, and attributes of complex community colleges are not simply additive; they derive from a host of factors that interact with one another, so simply tallying program review results would give a false picture of overall quality.

In this era of accountability, shrinking financial resources, and greater urgency for community colleges to remain flexible and responsive, program review can inform institutional leaders about what needs to be enriched, revised, improved, maintained, downsized, and even eliminated. From this perspective, program review can be frightening to those within the unit. As much as a college views program review as a means to quality improvement, honest reviews can have negative consequences for those within the unit, especially if the unit's performance is gauged to be inadequate or the expense of sustaining the unit is judged to outweigh the value of having it. I put this caveat near the beginning of this chapter because it is like the elephant in the room: the fear that everyone knows is there and no one will acknowledge or confront.

At the same time, program review offers units and the institution the opportunity to gather and analyze data and information to generate a realistic picture of the unit in order to identify strengths and weaknesses. The best use of program review is to turn to the results for improvement, and it is in that spirit that I continue this chapter.

Purposes of Program Review

Program review serves a number of purposes, some more obvious than others. At their best, reviews are a vehicle for enhancing a unit's knowledge of itself, including its place in the institution and how it serves its internal and external constituencies. This knowledge then becomes the basis for developing plans for improvement and ensuring that existing strengths are sustained. The latter point is often forgotten: attention is paid to weaknesses, but through inadvertent neglect, strengths can erode. Reviews support institutional planning and decision making regarding the continuing need for programs, maintaining and enhancing quality, developing and administering budgets, and eliminating programs that no longer have sufficient demand or quality or are not cost-effective. Reviews permit programs to identify best practices. From an institution-wide perspective, the value of best practices occurring within units can be leveraged and strengthened through sharing information throughout the organization.

Program review conducted for intelligence and improvement can be formative or summative in emphasis. Formative reviews are done while a program is ongoing and permit midprogram corrections. Summative reviews are conducted at the completion of a program and permit evaluating overall effectiveness and the achievement of goals. Although formative and summative reviews tie to specific time periods or key dates in the life of a program, most units at a community college will continue to be in existence after the program review is completed, so that the review can be perceived as having elements of both formative and summative reviews. The formative element places emphasis on identifying what is working and what is not and how the program can improve. The summative review emphasizes a more comprehensive perspective of the unit and may focus especially on some discrete projects or programs within the program whose continuation is not certain because of funding considerations or a clear timetable for termination such as in a two-year pilot project. Summative reviews are also conducted for external purposes such as accreditation or accountability.

Several factors reinforce the perception that program reviews are summative rather than formative. One is the sense at many institutions that reviews are focused on conclusions about the program rather than indicators suggesting program improvement. A second is that in today's climate of accountability, program reviews are frequently viewed as a vehicle for demonstrating achievements. Finally, although the cyclical nature of program review at many colleges ought to remind individuals that reviews are ongoing, the reality is that departments mobilize for program review and, when the year is over, demobilize and move on to other projects.

Meeting External Requirements and Expectations for Accountability. A second major purpose of program review is to meet external requirements and demands for accountability. Some states require colleges to conduct program reviews on a regular cycle, at least of instructional, if not of all, units. Specialized accreditation can be viewed as a distinctive form of program review because agencies typically require a program seeking accreditation to conduct a self-study aligned with the accrediting agency's criteria and guidelines. Except for accreditation, where minimum standards of performance are expected to be met, external demands for accountability and program review may not establish thresholds of performance. Rather, what is desired is evidence that the institution engages in regularly scheduled self-examinations and reports data about performance measured on key performance indicators that may be defined by an external group such as a state agency, by the college itself, or by a combination of the two.

Neutralizing Interference.   The third broad purpose of program review is related to meeting external calls for accountability but is less obvious: to serve as a defense against intrusion by higher-level administration or boards of trustees within the college or by state governing boards and legislatures. By demonstrating a willingness to examine programs and make difficult decisions about program quality, continuation, or termination, a college is better positioned to make its own decisions rather than having someone else impose decisions. From the departmental perspective, raising questions about program viability and quality and developing plans for improvement may prevent higher-level administration from prescribing courses of action or at least foster partnerships between the department and administration to collaborate.

Public Relations.   Not often acknowledged, one of the purposes of program review can be to compile data and information to use in promoting a program, recruiting students, marketing the college, or marshaling evidence to support public campaigns for bond or tax referenda. Barak and Brier (1990) suggest that such reviews are generally self-serving and not well regarded.

Providing Legitimacy.   Barak and Brier (1990) note yet another purpose for program review that is highly political. Authoritative reviews, they say, are conducted primarily as expressions of power and may not be evaluative or useful. Reviews of this nature serve almost as clubs, reminding those within a department about who is in charge and pushing the agenda of individuals in positions of authority. Authoritative program reviews may be used to lend an air of legitimacy to decisions already made about program termination or reorganization.

Determining the Most Compelling Purposes.   A number of factors affect which program review purposes are most compelling: the culture of the institution and its history of engaging in self-analyses and continuous improvement; the nature of the environment within which the college operates, especially the degree of institutional autonomy from state-level coordination or governance; and the degree to which financial or political exigencies create pressure for change.

In the ideal world, program review is one of the key vehicles for implementing a quality improvement agenda. Although I acknowledge program review might be conducted for less-than-salutary purposes, the remainder of this chapter assumes reviews are done primarily for intelligence, improvement, and meeting external mandates, not for political or self-serving purposes.

Process and Product

By process, I mean the manner in which program reviews are conducted, including the people involved. Institutions generally have great flexibility in developing program review processes, which to be sustainable and useful need to align with the institution's culture and related activities. A number of factors influence the selection of a process. The leading factor is how the institution conceives of program review. If it is viewed as a type of self-study in which the unit must be centrally engaged, then the locus of the project must reside within the unit itself. If it is viewed as a compilation of data and information about a unit, then the process may reside within the one or two offices responsible for compiling the material.

A related factor is the institution's usual approach to addressing issues. For example, a college that ordinarily convenes broad-based committees to address issues or has a strong tradition of shared governance may find a college-wide program review committee to be appropriate. An institution that is accustomed to having functional units such as academic and student affairs operate with relative autonomy may find it awkward and uncomfortable to bring multiple perspectives to the program review table.

A third factor is the centrality of program review to the decision-making process. If outcomes of program review have high stakes—they lead to decisions about the future of the program and its place in the institution—then gathering information from across the institution may help to enrich information and knowledge about the program. If, however, program review is a sidebar to decision making, conducted, for example, solely to meet state requirements, then involving more than a handful of individuals may not be a good use of staff time and energy. A fourth factor is the alignment of program review with other activities such as reaccreditation studies, strategic planning, or staff reorganizations. These types of activities, as well as program reviews, typically occur periodically rather than annually, and results of program reviews can inform them, especially if the review process is consciously crafted with this purpose in mind and on a timetable where reviews precede decisions. A fifth factor affecting the program review process is the perspective of what the reviews should contain. If they consist exclusively or primarily of quantitative data supplied by a handful of offices, such as institutional research and the budget office, then the process may require heavy investment by those offices and relatively little effort on the part of others. But if the content is broader, requiring departments to look at a wide range of data and information, conduct special studies, seek input from internal and external stakeholders, and bring state and national information into the examination of a program, then the process will need to involve more people and probably extend over a longer period of time.

By product, I mean the report or reports produced as a result of program review. The product may be a paper report, a Web page, an oral presentation, or any combination of these. Products may include narrative sections, graphic depictions of data, copies of department publications, screen shots of department Web sites, transcripts or excerpts of interviews with students or other constituencies, and financial audits. As with process, program review products vary. Some colleges want long narratives that permit the unit to present a wealth of data and information; others narrow the product to a few pages of quantitative data depicting performance on key indicators; and still others allow latitude, letting each unit decide how to present program review results.

What Can Be Learned

A comprehensive program review will result in data and information about a wide variety of department attributes. Although the following list is not exhaustive, it illustrates the types of insights that can be gained:

Program description: A clear account of the current status of the program, including its mission, purposes, and the extent to which it is achieving program goals and objectives. Inviting members of the unit to participate in developing the description can be a useful approach for generating discussions about the unit; often unit members are so busy with day-to-day operations they fail to consider the overarching reasons for the unit's existence, its primary constituencies, and what indicators ought to be used to measure the quality of performance.

SWOT (strengths, weaknesses, opportunities, threats): Identification of program strengths, weaknesses, opportunities, and threats, including those external and internal to the college. The analysis can sharpen understanding of the nature of weaknesses and how, or even whether, they can be addressed. The analysis can also heighten awareness of the institutional and external environments within which the unit operates and how environmental factors affect the unit. Finally, opportunities for program growth and development may be identified through the analysis.

Unique program attributes: Characteristics of the program that make it unique or distinctive within the institution, regionally or nationally. External grants, awards from professional organizations, and novel curricula or services are among the types of evidence that support assertions of uniqueness.

Organizational dependencies: Explication of how the program is linked to other programs and services within the institution, including how the program's functioning relies on the provision of resources and assistance from other units, as well as how the program under consideration provides essential resources and assistance elsewhere.

Resource use: Compilation of data and understanding of the program's costs and revenues, including external grants, donations, in-kind contributions, and partnerships. The college's expectations regarding the extent to which programs should be self-supporting or subsidized by institutional funds will shape conclusions about whether resource use is appropriate and sustainable.

Process efficiencies: Compilation and analysis of data regarding the efficiencies and resource use of the program, including faculty loads, class sizes, and facilities use for instructional programs; use and outcomes of, and facilities dedicated to, student support services; and productivity of and facilities allocated to administrative units.

Program outcomes: Data and analysis demonstrating the extent to which desired program outcomes are being attained. Outcomes examples include students' meeting learning objectives, degree completions, net revenues after costs, average class size, wait time before a service transaction is executed, and employer satisfaction with graduates.

Key issues and institutional priorities: How the program is responding to key issues and helping the institution move forward to attain priorities. Examples include responding to budget reductions or unexpected enrollment growth, increasing institutional diversity, increasing the percentage of students passing gatekeeper courses, and recruiting students from underrepresented groups.

Improvement: Plans for addressing weaknesses and sustaining strengths, including necessary resources (budget, staff, space, equipment, marketing) to implement plans and how implementation will be evaluated.

Models of Program Review

I present several of the many models and variations of program reviews, recognizing that most reviews contain elements of more than one model. The choice of which model to use at a college depends on a number of factors, including institutional culture, availability of technical and data compilation support, external program review reporting requirements, and other processes to evaluate programs in place at the organization.

Standardized Program Review. A standardized program review is primarily quantitative, with program performance indicators compiled in the same way, insofar as possible, for all programs. Often standardized reviews are completed annually for all programs, and data presentations might take the form of dashboards or balanced scorecards. Arrows or colors draw attention to measures on which the program moved up or down over previous years, are above or below the means of comparative programs, or meet or fail to meet a program target. Common measures for instructional programs include course enrollments, credit hours generated, full-time-equivalent (FTE) students, FTE faculty, number or percentage of courses and credits taught by full-time and part-time faculty, degree completion numbers or rates, program revenues and costs, and student and employer satisfaction. Noninstructional programs are less likely to use standardized program reviews because developing a common set of performance measures is more challenging. However, some measures can be used for most, if not all, instructional support and administrative units (for example, cost, customer satisfaction, utilization, number of transactions). Standardized program reviews can provide snapshots of programs as well as identify changes over time in the performance indicators. They are less able to depict and foster evaluations based on unique program characteristics or special circumstances affecting the program.

Free-Form Program Review.   A free-form program review is one in which each unit develops its own set of data to examine, its own mode for presenting quantitative and qualitative data, and its own array of supporting documents. This kind of review can be especially difficult for college leadership to use since little commonality among reviews is likely to exist, and the comprehensiveness of the review will vary across units since there are no common guidelines or expectations.

External Evaluation or Self-Study Focus Program Review.   These reviews align in format and content with requirements of external agencies. Such agencies often have specific criteria or quality indicators used to evaluate a program. The most obvious reviews with an external evaluation focus are those used to seek or maintain specialized program accreditation. The regional accrediting agencies' accreditation documents and processes are typically too broad to substitute for a program review, although the contents of program reviews may provide critical material for regional accreditation self-studies or compliance statements.

Outside Expert Program Review.   Some institutions retain outside experts to conduct program reviews. For example, a highly regarded political science faculty member in a similar institution might be hired to spend several days reviewing political science department documents, visiting on campus and then preparing a report about the program. While bringing in outside experts is intended to provide an objective assessment, two risks are particularly noteworthy: one is that a colleague from the same area will be reluctant to come forward with criticisms, thereby giving a superficial or unwarranted positive evaluation, and the other is that critical comments from an outsider may be greeted with defensiveness. A variation on the outside expert review is to have individuals from the program visit peer institutions to learn how similar colleges organize, deliver, fund, and evaluate comparable programs. Although representatives from the institution being visited will not provide observations about the program from which visitors come, their ideas and healthy exchanges of information can approximate an outside expert's guidance.

Another approach to bringing in data or information from outside is benchmarking: comparing the department's data with comparable data from peer institutions. Most community college benchmarking projects compile data at the institutional rather than the program or department level. However, some national surveys, such as the Community College Survey of Student Engagement, permit participating institutions to compare their results with those from peer institutions on selected topics that might align with program reviews; for example, student perceptions about orientation, college success courses, and financial aid may be relevant to program reviews in student affairs, departments offering success courses, and financial aid offices.

Mixed Program Reviews.   Many program reviews contain elements from most or all of the formats described. For example, the office of research might generate standard report elements at the program level (enrollments, average class size, percentage of credits taught by full- and part-time faculty) that become part of a program review report and that also contains descriptive information, results of special surveys or focus groups, faculty and staff perceptions of the program, and observations from outside experts invited to the campus.

Instructional and Noninstructional Unit Reviews

Many institutions review only their instructional programs; indeed, some limit these to career and technical education programs. The institution seeking to gain a comprehensive understanding of the organization—its processes and quality, challenges and strengths, and interdependencies among units—will benefit from extending program review to all areas.

While clearly academic and nonacademic units focus on different indicators of quality, efficiency, and effectiveness, the methods used to prepare and the format of the review can be the same, or nearly so. By sharing approaches and formats, colleagues from across the institution can coach and mentor one another through the process, as well as gain ideas about how to elicit perceptions from students, employees, and external stakeholders; how to present data and information without drowning in minutiae; how to write statements that provide evidence to support assertions of quality; and other aspects of the review process and product.

Many nonacademic units can draw from professional organizations for ideas about relevant measures and standards. For example, the Council for the Advancement of Standards in Higher Education (CAS) has developed standards for evaluating a number of functional areas that deliver student support services and for assessing student learning. The standards are purposely designed for institutions to use in studying themselves, and they represent what professionals in the field perceive as the essential characteristics of high-quality programs and services. Though typically thought to apply primarily to student affairs, the CAS standards and materials can be useful for academic programs as well.

Guiding Principles and the Link to Institutional Effectiveness

Barak and Brier (1990) set forth seven guiding principles for program reviews that continue to define successful processes and products:

- *Fairness.* All programs must be evaluated objectively if results are to be meaningful.
- *Comprehensiveness.* All aspects of all programs at all levels must be reviewed.
- *Timeliness.* All programs must be reviewed on a regular, predetermined basis.
- *Communication.* Throughout the entire process, people involved in the review and key figures in the institution must be kept fully informed of the review and its results.
- *Objectivity.* The design of the process and the selection of personnel must ensure as much objectivity as possible.
- *Credibility.* The process must be perceived as being fair and equitable to all programs.
- The results of the program review must be used in the planning and budgeting of the institution.

To Barak and Brier's principles I would add these:

- *Feasibility.* Expectations set for program reviews, both process and product, must align with resources available for conducting the review and other commitments of key personnel. Barak and Brier (1990) discuss feasibility as part of identifying the need for a review. I raise it to a guiding principle because the design and execution of reviews must be built on a clear understanding and institutional commitment of resources.
- *Sensible definitions.* What constitutes a program will need to be customized for the college. Sometimes it is clear, as in a nursing program. Other times it is less so: Is history a program, or does it reside within a larger social science program? Is a "program" the same as a "department"? Do budget configurations align with managerial ones? For example, a college might have a separate budget for chemistry and for physics but manage both through a single department chairperson who perceives both disciplines as combined. There is no single way to delineate programs; consequently, the college should define them in ways that make organizational sense.
- *Comparable, valid, and reliable data from a central source.* The institutional research and budget offices should provide data to departments to ensure the same operational definitions across units. For example, program enrollment can be defined many ways: number of students who have declared this to be their program of study; duplicated head count of enrollments in courses; unduplicated number of students taking one or more courses in the program; full-time equivalent students (credits divided by twelve or fifteen). To complicate the data further, the timing of the enrollment count must be clear; for example, are these enrollments at the census date, the end of the semester, or some other

key point in the term? If departments count students differently, the institutional value of program reviews will be diminished.

- *Training.* Many faculty and staff are unfamiliar with how to use data and information to illuminate and analyze programs, or the many types of evidence that can be used to evaluate a program. They may not know how to write an objective narrative, differentiate between feelings and facts about a program, or develop measurable student outcomes. Training can help them overcome insecurity about conducting the review and improve the quality of the final product.

Program reviews provide information and evidence about institutional effectiveness, but some of the most frequently used indicators of institutional effectiveness are measured at the institutional, and not the program, level. For example, the National Community College Benchmarking Project uses a number of familiar performance indicators at the institutional level, such as student engagement, student performance at transfer institutions, credit students who enrolled fall to spring and fall to fall, and institution-wide credit grades. Other of its indicators can be reduced to the program level, including number of graduates, success of developmental students in developmental and first-level college courses, and career program completers. However, few community colleges expect each program to be accountable for the performance of students in that program except in courses within the program itself and for degree or certificate completion. Community colleges instead take a broader view and expect the college to take primary ownership for student success. The exception is in health career and some other limited-enrollment programs where students are clearly identified and move through the curriculum mostly as a cohort.

Program reviews concentrate on units within the institution, and institutional effectiveness concentrates holistically on the organization. Put another way, program review focuses on the microlevel and institutional effectiveness on the macrolevel. Neither supplants or replaces the other. Both are important for a comprehensive understanding of quality at a community college, and both point to opportunities for improvement as well as strengths to be nurtured and sustained.

Reference

Barak, R. J., and Brier, B. E. *Successful Program Review.* San Francisco: Jossey-Bass, 1990.

TRUDY BERS is executive director of institutional research, curriculum, and strategic planning at Oakton Community College in Des Plaines, Illinois.

This chapter presents commonly used measures of student success, analyzes their strengths and weaknesses, and discusses innovative measures being used to benchmark community colleges throughout the United States.

Measuring Student Success

Christopher Baldwin, Estela Mara Bensimon, Alicia C. Dowd,
Lisa Kleiman

Student success is at the heart of both institutional effectiveness and the community college mission, yet measuring such success at community colleges is problematic. This chapter highlights three efforts to grapple with this problem—a multistate work group of system- and state-level policymakers to create an improved set of student success measures to gauge state and institutional performance; the development of benchmarking tools to improve racial/ethnic equity in college student outcomes and improve evaluation of institutional effectiveness in promoting student success; and an example of how one institution is leveraging state, regional, and national efforts to more effectively measure, and ultimately improve, student outcomes. Through these examples, we present the commonly used measures of student success, analyze their strengths and weaknesses, and discuss innovative measures that are being used to benchmark community colleges.

State Efforts to Use Better Measures to Drive Innovation and Improvement

Achieving the Dream: Community Colleges Count is a national initiative to help more community college students succeed, particularly students of color and low-income status. The initiative operates on multiple fronts, including efforts on campuses and in research, public engagement, and public policy, and emphasizes the use of data to drive change. Achieving

New Directions for Community Colleges, no. 153, Spring 2011 © 2011 Wiley Periodicals, Inc.
Published online in Wiley Online Library (wileyonlinelibrary.com) • DOI: 10.1002/cc.438

the Dream (ATD) was launched in 2004 with funding provided by the Lumina Foundation for Education. Seven national partner organizations work with Lumina to guide the initiative and provide technical and other support to the colleges and states. Jobs for the Future (JFF) coordinates the effort to improve policies in the sixteen states that are participating in ATD and also directs the work of the Cross-State Data Work Group.

In 2006, six states—Connecticut, Florida, North Carolina, Ohio, Texas, and Virginia—came together to develop, test, and pilot a better way of measuring community college performance. As the original participants in the Cross-State Data Work Group, these states have argued that the current federal approach to measuring community colleges is incomplete and that a better set of measures is needed to measure student progression and completion. Informed by the educational pipeline research of the National Center for Higher Education Management Systems (Ewell, 2006), the Washington State "tipping points" study conducted by the Community College Research Center (Prince and Jenkins, 2005), this group piloted a more robust approach for tracking community college students. This approach is delineated in a policy brief, *Test Drive: Six States Pilot Better Ways to Measure and Compare Community College Performance* (Goldberger and Gerwin, 2008). Essentially the brief recommends that the Integrated Postsecondary Educational Data System Graduation Rate Survey needs to be augmented to include part-time students, extend the period of time for tracking students from four to six years, and incorporate successful transfers to a four-year institutions as an outcome measure.

Since the publication of *Test Drive*, Arkansas, Massachusetts, Oklahoma, and Washington have joined the early participants, and the group has further refined the final outcomes measures. These states also developed a set of intermediate metrics, or milestones, that will help states and institutions track students' progression on their way toward successful completion of college. Starting with the foundation of identifying a more appropriate set of student success measures, the intermediate milestones were designed to answer some key questions:

• Are students being retained from term to term and year to year?
• What are the key credit thresholds that point to student progression and completion?
• Are students progressing through developmental education and into credit-bearing gatekeeper courses?
• Are students completing the gatekeeper courses within a certain period of time?

With these questions in mind, the states in the Cross-State Data Work Group labored for over a year to develop benchmarks for student success— a common set of final and intermediate measures with the consistent descriptions and data elements (Table 7.1). The group started by using

Table 7.1.   Achieving the Dream Cross-State Benchmarks
for Student Success

Final outcome measures (measured at the fourth and the sixth years)
Award of less than associate degree without transfer
Award of associate degree or higher without transfer
Award of less than associate degree and transferred
Award of associate degree or higher and transferred
Transferred without an award
Still enrolled with thirty or more college hours
Total success rate

First-year milestones
Persisted fall to spring
Passed 80 percent or more of attempted hours
Earned twenty-four or more hours

Second- and third-year milestones
Persisted fall to fall
Completed developmental math by year 2
Earned forty-eight or more hours
Passed gatekeeper English or higher by year 3
Passed gatekeeper math or higher by year 3

student-unit data to empirically test the impact of different measures on student success. For example, the group used Florida data to examine which credit thresholds were most predictive of student success at particular periods of time. After testing the measures empirically and coming to an agreement about cross-state definitions of the data elements, all members of the work group have run state-level aggregate analyses on the intermediate and final measures. The states have also disaggregated their analyses by subgroups that include age, enrollment status, level of college readiness, income (as measured by students receiving Pell grants), gender, and ethnicity.

Identifying the appropriate set of indicators for student success has been only part of the task of the Cross-State Data Work Group. Several states in the group have made substantial improvements in their technical and human data capacity by updating their data systems and hiring new staff. For example, Connecticut created an institutional research data mart to more effectively share data with its twelve community colleges. Leveraging national conversations about improving state data systems, the members of the work group recognized early on that meaningful improvements in student outcomes would be realized only if the state and institutional capacity to collect, analyze, and share data was strengthened. To guide discussions about data capacity, the work group also published a policy brief—*Power Tools: Designing State Community College Data and Performance Measurement System to Increase Student Success* (Goldberger,

2007)—that articulates the ideal components of a data and performance and measurement system and includes a self-assessment tool that states can use to gauge their own capacity.

Beyond the requisite technical and human capacity, many of the states in the data work group have developed innovative means for presenting and using their data to drive improvements, including publishing updated institutional comparisons on key measures of student success. The North Carolina Community College System regularly publishes the Data Trends series (www.nccommunitycolleges.edu/Reports/research.htm), which includes systemwide analyses of student success measures and institutional comparison data. The Florida Department of Education publishes *Fast Facts* (www.fldoe.org/cc/OSAS/FastFacts/FastFacts.asp) and *Zoom* (www.fldoe.org/cc/OSAS/Evaluations/zoom.asp), series of short summaries of recent research related to the Florida College System. Discussions about an improved approach to sharing success data spurred the Virginia Community College System to begin publishing the bimonthly *Student Success Snapshot* (www.vccs.edu/Default.aspx?tabid=622) in 2008 that benchmarks all community colleges on a specific success measure in each issue. These short reports are regularly shared with college presidents, state policymakers, and the public. The Texas Higher Education Coordinating Board posts on its accountability Web site disaggregate data on a set of student success measures for the state's community colleges (www.txhighereddata.org/Interactive/AccountabilityDRAFT/). The board provides all two-year institutions with reports on the academic performance of transfer students at Texas public universities, as well as information on employment and additional education that former students pursue.

The Achieving the Dream state teams have cited the substantial value of continued cross-state conversations, particularly the efforts of the Cross-State Data Work Group. The state data leads involved in this group have formed a powerful network that provides them with an opportunity to learn from each other's experiences and to convey their progress and challenges to others. The cross-state conversation around a common set of measures fosters ongoing dialogue about different state policy priorities and their impact on student progression and success. The consistent cross-state approach of this effort gives its benchmarks for student success substantial weight and credibility as national deliberations such as development of the Voluntary Framework of Accountability for community colleges play out.

The most significant impact of this work has been within states. *Benchmarks for Student Success* establishes a common language and set of expectations that, when shared among institutions and publicly, makes student progression and outcomes more transparent. Using these measures can help practitioners identify promising practices among peer institutions and help state policymakers integrate lessons and findings into ongoing policy discussions. In 2009, the Bill and Melinda Gates Foundation funded the Developmental Education Initiative, which includes the original members of the data work group, to focus more deeply on improving outcomes for students who place into developmental education. The *Developmental Education Initiative: State Policy Framework and Strategy* (Jobs for the Future, 2010; www.deionline.org) includes a data-driven improvement process that makes the performance of institutions more transparent, recognizes colleges that are consistently reporting better student outcomes, and creates sustained peer networks of practitioners to learn from one another. States have a substantial and important role as conveners of their colleges to share knowledge and best practices and to scale promising innovations in the service of improved student outcomes. The measures developed by the Cross-State Data Work Group give states and institutions a powerful tool to facilitate these ongoing conversations.

Benchmarking for Organizational Learning and Change

Around the same time that the Lumina Foundation launched Achieving the Dream, the foundation also funded two action research projects: Equity for All at the University of Southern California's Center for Urban Education (CUE) and the Community College Student Success Project at the University of Massachusetts Boston.[1] These projects forwarded two important goals: to improve racial/ethnic equity in college student outcomes and improve evaluation of institutional effectiveness in promoting student success. Both focused on organizational learning, emphasizing that "data don't drive"; decision makers do (Dowd, 2005). The two projects advanced understanding of what is needed to create a culture of inquiry (*Creating a Culture of Inquiry*, 2005), including data tools and norms of professional practice where data are used systematically for problem solving.

By developing the tools and techniques for inquiry, these projects fostered the use of data for decision-making and organizational change. As the Cross-State Data Work Group, coordinated by JFF, developed data standards and the *Benchmarks for Student Success*, Equity for All, led by Estela Bensimon, the Community College Student Success Project, led by Alicia Dowd, collaborated with practitioners across the country to determine how these data could best be used for change in higher education (Bensimon, Rueda, Dowd, and Harris, 2007; Dowd, 2008; Dowd and Tong, 2007).

Equity for All involved approximately one hundred individuals from nine California community colleges who analyzed their college data for student retention, transfer, and degree completion. All data were disaggregated by race and ethnicity, and the results revealed inequities among racial/ethnic groups in higher education based on four perspectives represented on CUE's Equity Scorecard: access, retention, transfer, and institutional effectiveness. The Community College Student Success Project involved a dozen practitioners from Massachusetts and other New England states in a think tank to assess standards for institutional assessment, peer

benchmarking, and evaluation.[2] Another sixteen community college practitioners served as the project's national advisory board. The advisory board
met at conferences and symposia in 2004 and 2005 to inform the think
tank proceedings and the drafting of reports based on their experiences
with state policies, institutional assessment practices, and data systems
from across the country.

Through these highly collaborative processes of data analysis and discussion of data standards, it became clear that even when data gain credibility at the level of state or federal policy, much more work remains to be
done to motivate changes in college teaching, curriculum, and administration. The end users of the data need to be convinced that the problems
revealed by the data are "real" and that the users can do something to
address those problems. To build on what we learned through these two
projects about using data for decision making to improve equity and institutional effectiveness, we teamed up at the CUE in 2007 and 2008 and
launched the California Benchmarking Project.[3]

The purpose of the California Benchmarking Project was to foster
growth in equity-based, practitioner-driven assessment as a way to improve
community college student success across the entire curriculum, from basic
skills to transfer-level courses. CUE researchers partnered with community
college administrators, faculty, counselors, and institutional researchers.
Three colleges convened evidence teams of approximately twelve to sixteen
campus leaders at each college. These individuals participated in monthly
meetings and project symposia facilitated by CUE researchers. They collaborated with CUE in developing and testing the use of equity-based
assessment processes and tools. An additional 130 practitioners from
twenty-five California community colleges participated in symposia and
seminars hosted by CUE to pilot-test the equity-based assessment tools that
had been developed.

These methods and tools were organized using the concepts of
performance, diagnostic, and process benchmarking. These are briefly
described here to set the context of the findings (see Dowd and Tong,
2007, for more information; for an application to degree completion in
science, technology, engineering, and mathematics, see Dowd, Malcom,
and Bensimon, 2009).

Through performance benchmarking, we asked our community college partners to examine successful course completion data and entering
student cohort migration rates from basic skills classes to transfer classes,
disaggregated by race/ethnicity, and asked them to set performance goals
for the improvement of equity and effectiveness.

Through diagnostic benchmarking, we asked participants to use diagnostic indicators of equitable institutional performance to assess their
practices in basic skills education. The evidence teams discussed existing
standards of best practices and compared them to their own campus practices. They then reviewed best practice diagnostic indicators with a critical

eye to determine if they were likely to have a positive impact on racial/ethnic equity. CUE researchers drew on concepts of culturally responsive pedagogy, and we involved content-area experts in mathematics and composition in order to assess whether certain standards of practice were more inclusive than others of underrepresented students. The diagnostic benchmarking process involved data collection using protocols for on-campus observation, syllabi review, student assessment, and peer interviews.

For the purpose of process benchmarking, we facilitated hosted site visits for the evidence team members at peer colleges, which were selected through the diagnostic benchmarking step as having exemplary programs worthy of fuller understanding. The site visits enabled participants to learn strategic and operational details of organizational change processes that must be taken into account before adopting exemplary practices from another campus. For each site visit, CUE researchers created observation guides that helped prompt team members from each college to reflect on how to implement exemplary practices, such as in learning centers or student support programs on their campuses. In addition, the observation guide prompted team members to reflect on and discuss the benefits of the practices they observed and how these practices might or might not fit their campus culture and organizations.

All of these benchmarking activities engaged participants in a cycle of inquiry (illustrated in Figure 7.1) promoting reflection, goal setting, and expertise in problem solving to improve institutional equity and effectiveness. Through interviews with half of our inquiry team participants, we evaluated what the participants had experienced and learned through these types of benchmarking activities. The interviews were conducted using a semistructured interview protocol designed to elicit discussion about participants' motivations, reactions, experiences, learning, and behaviors.

Figure 7.1. California Benchmarking Project Benchmarking and Inquiry Process

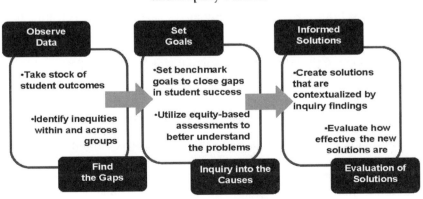

Evaluations administered to participants in benchmarking symposia indicated that participants valued what they learned. These results are important because they demonstrate that community college practitioners are open to learning about their own practices and roles as change agents through close examination of college data. Three-quarters or more of the respondents agreed or strongly agreed that (1) the benchmarking activities and materials provided were useful and facilitated their learning, (2) they were willing to share equity-based assessment strategies on their campuses, and (3) they were willing to implement benchmarking strategies at their community college. We also found an increased capacity for data-based decision making and a greater awareness of the issues of racial/ethnic equity in student outcomes.

The CUE's studies have generated greater understanding of how to move beyond espousing a culture of inquiry to creating one through the use of specific institutional assessment processes and tools. CUE researchers continue to refine the benchmarking processes we have developed in collaboration with community college practitioners to increase racial/ethnic equity in student outcomes and improve institutional effectiveness. Our results to date show that when administrators, student affairs professionals, and faculty use data tools such as CUE's Equity Scorecard and our Benchmarking Equity and Student Success Tool to make meaning of student outcome data, dialogue and knowledge of what the data say about institutional effectiveness are enhanced. Participants also gain a keener understanding of comparative standards of instructional quality through the diagnostic and process benchmarking activities. In our experience, this often leads to a greater willingness to experiment with new instructional strategies and administrative structures.

Today a great deal of emphasis is placed on developing higher education data systems to track student progress and educational achievement. There is also a growing awareness that data-driven decision making must be complemented by a culture of inquiry. Practitioners need to be able to ask the right questions of available data and make changes in their educational practices as a result of what they learn. The CUE's work supports both of these priorities. Most other initiatives have focused on creating data standards and performance benchmarking indicators. With that foundation, greater attention can now be paid to using diagnostic and process benchmarking to promote organizational learning and change.

Tidewater Community College Student Success Initiatives

In addition to participating in Achieving the Dream: Community Colleges Count, over the past several years, Tidewater Community College (TCC) in Norfolk, Virginia, launched several major initiatives centered on student success, including a Title III grant, the college's SACS Quality Enhancement

Plan (QEP), and a Virginia Community College System strategic plan. Each had a slightly different overall focus to help improve student success. As the institutional effectiveness (IE) office collected vast amounts of data in support of each effort, it became apparent that the college needed a plan to address student success in a way that made sense given the student population, and that it would be understandable to the college community at large, as well as the general public.

Most commonly used measures of student success have limitations primarily because graduation and retention rates have been defined historically in terms of traditional four-year student enrollment patterns. Federal graduation and retention rates exclude 65 percent or more of TCC's student body and fail to recognize students enrolled part time, those needing remedial work, or those who transfer or take a job prior to completing a degree. Pat Stanley, deputy assistant secretary for community colleges in the US Department of Education, remarked that the traditional student is as irrelevant today as the traditional family (Stanley, 2008). Ultimately success defined for TCC students is very different from student success defined for a highly selective four-year institution.

During the course of 2008-2009, TCC's IE office completed a literature review, examined student outcomes from the student success initiatives, and engaged the college leadership in dialogue about student success. As the college embarked on creating a new model for student success, four principles guided the work:

- To be inclusive rather than exclusive
- To acknowledge the difference in community college student enrollment patterns as compared to four-year traditional student patterns
- To expand the definition of success to recognize the mission of the community college and embrace the notion of open door institutions
- To better understand the intent and educational goals of the community college student

The new model was based on several underlying assumptions:

- That students enrolled in transfer or career and technical programs intend to complete the appropriate degree or award
- That students requiring developmental studies must progress to college-level math and English and successfully complete college-level course work to attain a degree
- That retention is the key to success:
  - Retention from the beginning to the end of each class period
  - Retention from the first semester to the second semester
  - Retention from the first year to the second year

The culmination of this work was a new definition for student success: achievement of an academic credential for program-placed students or the progression toward the credential within four years, to include students who have transferred prior to degree attainment or are still enrolled at the institution. Essentially TCC's student success definition recognized the diversity of the population, student enrollment patterns, and the role that the community college plays in the transfer process. The TCC student success model is built on three key elements—graduation, transfer out, and continued enrollment. Ultimately the sum of the three indicators is defined as TCC's advancement rate.

TCC's student success plan is grounded in a series of nine indicators that inform student success and are tracked over five years. Each indicator is measured every semester and has an annual target to reach the goal set for 2011-2112. The first indicator is the successful completion of a student development course within the first year of enrollment. There are also indicators for the successful completion of developmental math, college-level math, developmental English, college-level English, General Biology, General Chemistry, and online courses. The last three indicators are related to high-risk courses with low success rates. The ninth indicator is the completion of a newly implemented general education certificate, a milestone for those planning to complete the associate degree.

Cohorts of first-time, program-placed students are tracked over the course of four years to determine if they have graduated, have transferred out, or are still enrolled. Placement in any of the three categories is considered to be advancement toward a goal. In this case, enrollment patterns of most students are taken into account, and each cohort is inclusive of developmental and part-time students. As the nine indicator scores improve, the retention, graduation, and transfer-out rates are expected to improve. Each indicator is tracked in an annual scorecard, and the advancement rate is tracked annually as well. The advantage of the scorecard is that it shows if the advancement rate is improving. Annual tracking allows tracking along the four-year continuum and the opportunity to see if gains are being made each year. As Table 7.2 shows, the college advancement rate combines the nine indicators across time into an overall measure of student success.[4]

The indicators are what one would call leading indicators in economic theory. That is, they signal a future direction for the advancement rate. The indicators tend to increase or decrease before the advancement rate increases or decreases. For example, as the success rate for college-level English and math increases, one would expect to see the retention, and ultimately the graduation rate, increase at a future time. All degrees require college-level English, and increasing success rates should signal that more students are eligible to graduate. Similarly, if the successful completion of the student development course increases, one would expect to see the retention rate and the success rate in required courses increase in the near future. TCC's research showed a dramatic difference in successful comple-

Table 7.2 College Advancement Rate

	2007-08 Advancement Rate (Fall 2004 cohort)	2008-09 Advancement Rate (Fall 2005 cohort)	2009-10 Advancement Rate (Fall 2006 cohort)	2010-11 Advancement Rate (Fall 2007 cohort)
Year 1				
Graduated	0.8%	0.6%	0.1%	0.5%
Still Enrolled	52.9%	51.3%	54.0%	56.2%
Transferred	2.0%	5.2%	5.4%	7.1%
1-year Rate	**55.6%**	**57.1%** ↑	**59.5%** ↑	**63.8%** ↑
Year 2				
Graduated	4.5%	4.8%	4.5%	4.1%
Still Enrolled	32.8%	31.7%	36.6%	36.4%
Transferred	8.3%	10.6%	12.5%	13.6%
2-year Rate	**45.5%**	**47.1%** ↑	**53.6%** ↑	**54.1%** ↑
Year 3				
Graduated	9.9%	10.3%	11.1%	Sep 10
Still Enrolled	19.9%	19.9%	23.0%	Sep 10
Transferred	13.6%	16.4%	18.0%	Jan 11
3-year Rate	**43.4%**	**46.6%** ↑	**52.1%** ↑	Jan 11
Year 4				
Graduated	13.4%	14.2%	Sep 10	Sep 11
Still Enrolled	13.0%	13.4%	Sep 10	Sep 11
Transferred	14.3%	20.2%	Jan 11	Jan 12
4-year Rate	**40.7%**	**47.8%** ↑	Jan 11	Jan 12

New Directions for Community Colleges • DOI: 10.1002/cc

tion rates for the first English course for those who completed the student development course (71 percent) and those who did not (59 percent). A similar difference played out for successful completion of the first math course for those who completed the student development course (59 percent versus 41 percent).

Although the IE office can help inform policies related to student success through meaningful data analyses, the real change must happen at the campus level and in the classroom. A cultural shift must occur from the right-to-fail mentality of the previous century to the right-to-succeed mentality of this century. Although the college has made gains over the past five years and has cast a spotlight on student progress, much work remains to be done. Some of the strategies employed include a more effective student orientation system, with attention to first-year students, better connections to public school systems to improve college readiness efforts, early intervention for academically challenged students, outreach to students with many accumulated credits, and implementation of milestones such as the General Education Certificate to encourage student progression to a final goal.

The key to effecting change is dialogue. Faculty must engage in discussion across the disciplines; student services staff should be immersed in discussing new ways to accommodate growing numbers of students through technology and other innovative methods; and college leaders should be engaged in national discussions to help foster direction and understanding of community colleges and their mission. Widespread discussion is essential to the discovery of new strategies and effective delivery methods that can improve education in the twenty-first century.

Conclusion

No one formula ensures student success. While the basics may be the same across various institutions, no single plan can guarantee success in all community colleges. Each institution must know the population it serves and develop strategies and plans that complement the political realities and technical capacities of each state and school. Moving the numbers will not happen in a semester or a year. But by engaging in the discussion at local, state, and national levels, community college professionals can be part of the solution and help educate the public about the role of community colleges and those they serve. Finally, change happens in a classroom, not a boardroom. Faculty and staff must be key players in the dialogue on student success and be empowered to address barriers to success. Broad-based campus involvement, data-based improvement plans, and accountability measures grounded in meaningful data analysis are solid ingredients for a good start. Campus culture must be transformed to one where the community truly believes in the right to succeed.

NEW DIRECTIONS FOR COMMUNITY COLLEGES • DOI: 10.1002/cc

Notes

1. Equity for All was also funded by the Chancellor's Office of the California Community Colleges.
2. The think tank was hosted by the New England Resource Center for Higher Education at the University of Massachusetts Boston.
3. In 2007-2008, the William and Flora Hewlett Foundation and the Ford Foundation funded the Center for Urban Education to develop tools and processes for benchmarking equity and effectiveness through the center's California Benchmarking Project.
4. The College Advancement Rate is based somewhat loosely on the work of the Joint Commission on Accountability Reporting, which developed a student advancement rate in the mid-1990s. See Head (1995) and Joint Commission on Accountability Reporting (1996).

References

Bensimon, E. M., Rueda, R., Dowd, A. C., and Harris III, F. "Accountability, Equity, and Practitioner Learning and Change." *Metropolitan*, 2007, *18*(3), 28–45.

Center for Community College Student Engagement. *Benchmarking and Benchmarks: Effective Practice with Entering Students.* Retrieved from http://www.nisod.org/uploads /waiwaiole_9551_4.pdf on February 1, 2011.

Dowd, A. C. *Data Don't Drive: Building a Practitioner-Driven Culture of Inquiry to Assess Community College Performance.* Indianapolis, Ind.: Lumina Foundation for Education, 2005.

Dowd, A. C. "The Community College as Gateway and Gatekeeper: Moving Beyond the Access 'Saga' to Outcome Equity." *Harvard Educational Review,* 2008, *77*(4), 407–419.

Dowd, A. C., Malcom, L. E., and Bensimon, E. M. *Benchmarking the Success of Latina and Latino Students in STEM to Achieve National Graduation Goals.* Los Angeles: Center for Urban Education, University of Southern California, 2009.

Dowd, A. C., and Tong, V. P. "Accountability, Assessment, and the Scholarship of 'Best Practice.'" In J. C. Smart (ed.), *Handbook of Higher Education.* New York: Springer Publishing, 2007.

Ewell, P. "Reaching Consensus on Common Indicators: A Feasibility Analysis." Paper presented at the meeting of State Student Data Project for Community College Bridges to Opportunity and Achieving the Dream, San Antonio, Tex., 2006.

Goldberger, S. *Power Tools: Designing State Community College Data and Performance Measurement Systems to Increase Student Success.* Boston: Jobs for the Future, 2007.

Goldberger, S., and Gerwin, C. *Test Drive: Six States Pilot Better Ways to Measure and Compare Community College Performance.* Boston: Jobs for the Future, 2008.

Head, R. "Accountability Reporting: JCAR Student Success, Persistence, Transfer, Graduation and Licensure Rates." Paper presented at the Joint Commission on Accountability Reporting, Washington, D.C., Oct. 1995.

Jobs for the Future. *The Developmental Education Initiative: State Policy Framework and Strategy.* Boston: Jobs for the Future, 2010.

Joint Commission on Accountability Reporting. *CAR Technical Conventions Manual.* Washington, D.C.: American Association of States Colleges and Universities, American Association of Community Colleges, and National Association of State Universities and Land-Grant Colleges, 1996. Retrieved from http://www.aascu.org/pdf/jcar _technical.pdf on February 1, 2011.

New England Resource Center for Higher Education. "Creating a Culture of Inquiry." Boston: New England Resource Center for Higher Education, 2005.

Prince, D., and Jenkins, D. *Building Pathways to Success for Low-Skill Adult Students: Lessons for Community College Policy and Practice from a Statewide Longitudinal Tracking Study.* New York: Community College Research Center, Teachers College, Columbia University, 2005.

Stanley, P. "Creating a Culture of Evidence." Paper presented at the Southeastern Association of Community College Research Conference, St. Petersburg, Fla., Aug. 2008.

CHRISTOPHER BALDWIN *is a program director at Jobs for the Future in Boston.*

ESTELA MARA BENSIMON *is professor of higher education and codirector of the Center for Urban Education at the University of Southern California.*

ALICIA C. DOWD *is associate professor of higher education and codirector of the Center for Urban Education at the University of Southern California.*

LISA KLEIMAN *recently retired after thirty years as the founding director of institutional effectiveness at Tidewater Community College in Norfolk, Virginia.*

8

Policymakers, administrators, and institutional researchers should recognize the critical stakeholders in the area of institutional effectiveness at the community college, their differences in perceptions about institutional effectiveness, and ways to negotiate these differences in perception.

Stakeholders in the Institutional Effectiveness Process

Willard C. Hom

This chapter identifies the different stakeholders in the community college, notes how each views institutional effectiveness, and comments on opportunities arising from their different perspectives on institutional effectiveness. For this chapter, a stakeholder is broadly defined as a person or entity with an interest in some process, concept, or object.

This definition enables us to identify the basic kinds of stakeholders in institutional effectiveness. For simplicity, these stakeholders can be enumerated as members of two major groups: the on-campus group and the off-campus group. In the on-campus group are administrators, administrative staff, institutional researchers, faculty, students, and local trustees (trustees can also be considered to be in the off-campus group). In the off-campus group are accrediting commissions, government oversight and funding bodies, potential students, employers, baccalaureate institutions, K-12 officials and staff, external researchers (in either policy groups or university departments or programs), taxpayers (and their advocacy groups), and the news media. Although I could probably expand this enumeration to cover other parties (for example, a state's governor and legislators), this list covers the individuals who usually have the most interest in the concept of institutional effectiveness.

These identified groups need additional breakdown because individuals within them tend to have different levels of interest in institutional effectiveness. It is helpful to categorize these parties according to their

New Directions for Community Colleges, no. 153, Spring 2011 © 2011 Wiley Periodicals, Inc.
Published online in Wiley Online Library (wileyonlinelibrary.com) • DOI: 10.1002/cc.439

Table 8.1.   Categorization of Stakeholders

Categorization	High Authority	Low Authority
High interest	Community college administrators Trustees State oversight and budget bodies Accrediting commissions	Institutional researchers
Medium interest		Students (current and potential) Administrative staff Employers External researchers Baccalaureate institutions
Low interest		News media Faculty K–12 officials Taxpayers

levels of interest and their levels of authority over institutional policy to help us in understanding the viewpoints of different stakeholders. In general, stakeholders who have a low level of interest in institutional effectiveness tend also to have the least detailed and the least informed perception of institutional effectiveness. Table 8.1 shows the resulting categorization. The category for parties who presumably have both a high level of interest in institutional effectiveness and a high level of authority to affect institutional effectiveness includes community college administrators, trustees of local governing boards, state oversight and funding bodies, and accrediting commissions. The category with high interest but low authority includes institutional researchers at the community college.

Potential students, current students, administrative staff, employers, external researchers, and baccalaureate institutions are parties with typically medium levels of interest but low authority. These parties have a medium level of interest because as individual actors, they can benefit from knowledge about institutional effectiveness, but each one has many other sources of concern (that is, institutional effectiveness generally does not dominate their individual agendas). At the same time, none of these stakeholders holds any formal authority over institutions to influence their effectiveness. For example, an employer must focus on its revenue stream (its markets), and it generally has options other than the nearest community college for obtaining a labor force and a greater interest in a specific program (such as culinary arts) at a college than in the community college as a whole. In addition, an employer lacks formal authority over the institution; it influences institutional policy only through advisory groups and its labor market practices (that is, the hiring of community college students).

The category of low interest and low authority includes faculty, the news media, K-12 officials, and taxpayers. The faculty are in this category because instructors generally focus their attention on their immediate discipline rather than the entire institution. Faculty (aside from those who become involved in institution-wide groups like academic senates and accreditation teams) generally feel insulated from any commotion over the broad concept of institutional effectiveness, and individual instructors usually lack authority to alter institutional effectiveness, especially when the measurement of institutional effectiveness has an esoteric nature for them. Anecdotal evidence indicates that many faculty members may also hold unique perceptions about institutional effectiveness. For instance, many would place less weight on traditional quantitative measures of educational outcomes (such as degrees completed or transfers) and more weight on qualitative feedback (such as personal growth, intellectual growth, and civic engagement). At the same time, other faculty members would argue that institutional effectiveness is a holistic concept that should include hard-to-measure properties such as contributions to community culture and health and that it is impossible to achieve an accurate and affordable measure of institutional effectiveness.

The news media are in this category with faculty because these media (excluding industry-specific media like the *Chronicle of Higher Education*) have many stories and topics to cover with their limited resources and the effectiveness of community colleges is not sensational enough to capture the attention of the general public. Nonetheless, both the news media and faculty can wield immense influence (that is, informal power), rather than authority, to alter institutional policy and behavior despite their placement in Table 8.1. Thus, our categorization of the faculty and the news media may understate the potential influence of these two groups. K-12 officials are in this category because they generally must focus on their own system of institutional effectiveness. Although these officials may have an interest in community colleges, their interests tend to be narrow in scope for programs such as concurrent enrollment and occupational programs. Taxpayers and their advocacy groups fall into this group because they must allocate their attention and resources to a multitude of other public agencies that tend to consume a larger share of tax dollars. In addition, taxpayers, unless they or their family members enroll at a community college, tend to have little concern about institutional effectiveness. Furthermore, taxpayers tend to have only modest indirect authority through their votes on college trustees, community college-related bond measures, and state elections and state referenda.

Forces Behind Variation in Perceptions of Institutional Effectiveness

Thus far, our attention has focused on the identification of different stakeholders. We now look at how these different stakeholders may perceive the

Figure 8.1. Factors Influencing the Perception of
Institutional Effectiveness

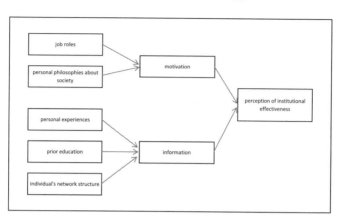

concept of institutional effectiveness. Based on my experience with these stakeholders, I propose a model of perception formation that appears in Figure 8.1. The most basic factors in this model are motivation and information.

For motivation, the subfactors are job role and personal philosophies about society. Job role theoretically has a salient effect because an individual usually adopts the perception that agrees with the assumptions of a specific job. For example, a job role of counseling for transfer would tend to give that counselor strong motivation to view the performance of the institution mainly in terms of its success in transferring students to baccalaureate institutions. Personal philosophies about society theoretically will shape the perception of institutional effectiveness because these beliefs tend to define for individuals the ideal roles for the community college. For example, a personal philosophy about society, such as a belief in the public's obligation for service to the disadvantaged, will tend to make an institution's performance in advancing the education of people with severe challenges the focal point of a perception about institutional effectiveness. Similarly, someone whose educational philosophy embraces progressivism would be more interested in the students than the curriculum, whereas one embracing realism would be more interested in the dissemination of knowledge.

For the information factor, the subfactors are personal experiences, prior education, and network structure. Personal experiences will shape a person's perception of institutional effectiveness because these experiences raise awareness for certain factors in an individual's perception of institutional effectiveness. Prior education will shape perception because it can create preferences for certain kinds of evidence, such as quantitative evidence or economic data. Finally, an individual's network structure will shape perception because a communication network can bring about peer influence and access to institutional data.

This basic model simplifies reality in a variety of ways. An individual can readily have more than one stakeholder role. For example, a faculty member may simultaneously serve as a dean of an academic program, prompting this individual to hold multiple perceptions of institutional effectiveness. Even when an individual maintains only one stakeholder role, he or she may harbor multiple perceptions of institutional effectiveness at a given point in time. An individual who has both multiple stakeholder roles and multiple perceptions of institutional effectiveness can switch to the specific perception that agrees most with the stakeholder role that he or she has at a particular time and place. For example, we can envision a college president who chooses to espouse a particular measure of institutional effectiveness because it may result in a more positive reputation for the college than he or she would conclude with other available measures of institutional effectiveness. This would agree with the president's job role to promote the community college, which entails securing public support and funding. This same individual may also hold a different perception—one that is critical of and negative to other community colleges—if he or she is serving on some oversight or accrediting body. Of course, some individuals may consider one specific perception as dominant in its weight such that he or she will maintain that perception regardless of different job roles. Finally, a subfactor may influence another subfactor, and a subfactor for information could influence motivation (and vice versa) as well. The model in Figure 8.1 therefore is a simplification of the real world.

Comparison of Stakeholder Perceptions

Psychological research provides a model that can help capture the complex nature of perceptions of institutional effectiveness. Multiattribute utility technology (MAUT) structures how individuals can evaluate a product or service by integrating evidence about different dimensions (multiple attributes) of a product or service (Edwards and Newman, 2000). I will avoid a technical discussion of MAUT because I borrow only the basic concept for this discussion. The following paragraphs demonstrate how individuals tend to consider a set of attributes when they judge the value or performance of something like a community college. As a didactic exercise, consider a hypothetical MAUT model for a college president and then, for comparison, a hypothetical MAUT model for an employer.

The MAUT model uses a graph known as a value tree to display its result, and this discussion will use such a display. Figure 8.2 is the value tree for a hypothetical college president. It presents this hypothetical case for didactic purposes only, and the choice of attributes and attribute weights is simply my guess of how a president may think. A value tree

Figure 8.2. Value Tree for a Hypothetical College President

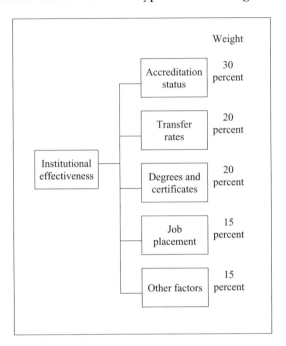

includes weights for each attribute, and Figure 8.2 includes hypothetical values for this example. It shows four major attributes and a set of other attributes that are too small to display separately. The value tree shows that the attribute of accreditation status carries the most weight in this hypothetical president's perception, at 30 percent of the total influence. Figure 8.3 is the corresponding value tree for a hypothetical employer. This hypothetical employer considers only two major attributes, job placement and accreditation, and weighs them at 50 percent and 30 percent, respectively.

A comparison of these two value trees shows how these two kinds of stakeholders differ in their perception of institutional effectiveness. The biggest difference lies in the attributes that each stakeholder considers. The other major difference lies in the weights that the stakeholders allot to the attributes that both individuals share (accreditation status and job placement).

Figures 8.2 and 8.3 elucidate how different stakeholders formulate divergent perceptions of institutional effectiveness. Some qualifying comments are in order, however. These models are static, but real-life perceptions can change as a function of the level of crystallization of individual beliefs and opinions and the change that may occur in the environment for an individual. Under certain circumstances, strong and sudden convergence in perceptions of institutional effectiveness can occur among different stakeholders. For example, if a college were to handle a serious campus security threat successfully, then almost all of the stakeholders will at least

Figure 8.3. Value Tree for a Hypothetical Employer

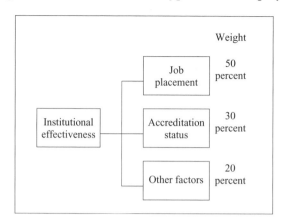

temporarily consider campus security a critical attribute in institutional effectiveness and assign a positive rating to that attribute. Finally, these examples of value trees are only didactic exercises; researchers who explore specific perceptions of stakeholders will need to survey the stakeholders of interest to them.

General Implications

The preceding discussion explains why and how different stakeholders develop different perceptions of institutional effectiveness. The existence of this spectrum of varied perceptions can hinder institutional improvement as well as help it. In terms of hindrance to improvement, differing perceptions of institutional effectiveness can act as potential obstacles to planning, decision making, and implementation. If stakeholders cannot reach agreement, then a group (such as a college's executive team or a board of trustees) may suffer gridlock by failing to define institutional effectiveness—a situation that would stymie coordinated efforts at institutional improvement. Even if stakeholders adopt a group-approved definition for institutional effectiveness (possibly by a majority vote), the underlying differences in perception that may linger despite a group decision can eventually lead to the subversion of resulting plans by dissident stakeholders. On occasion, if different conclusions about institutional effectiveness are publicly voiced by parties within the same college, this may weaken the credibility of the college, another administrative concern. In the special case where a college produces a numerical indicator of institutional effectiveness that differs in definition from that used in another study by a party that is independent of the college, allegations of deception or spin may arise if the college-produced indicator has a more positive result than the independently produced indicator.

One trend across the nation may also cause concern. Off-campus stakeholder pressure to make community colleges accountable may burden these institutions when oversight bodies require different measures of institutional effectiveness. With overloaded staff in research units and data processing units becoming the norm, this burden of multiple accountability reports can result in the neglect of other work that would benefit the college. And in some cases, there could arise a stressful competition for local resources between oversight stakeholders (accrediting commissions, boards of trustees, and state budgeting officials) because they all demand evidence to fulfill their separate accountability missions. At some point, this dilemma could result in a failure to satisfy the demands of one or more of these off-campus stakeholders. So divergence in perception can directly hinder administrative effort in a variety of ways.

Different perceptions of institutional effectiveness have special implications for analytical efforts that can indirectly hinder administrative effort. When different bodies use different perceptions of institutional effectiveness (and consequently different definitions), conflicting conclusions about institutional effectiveness may surface. For example, if a college did poorly in transferring students to baccalaureate institutions while it did well in job placement of associate degree or certificate completers, some of the college's trustees might consider the college as low performing (if they assumed that transfer was the primary mission) while others might view it as high performing (if they assumed that workforce development was the primary mission). It would not be surprising then that when legislators, trustees, or voters see such conflicting evidence, they may choose to delay or deny their support for an institution on the basis of their uncertainty about its effectiveness. If public officials evaluate institutional effectiveness through a comparison of similar colleges (a peer group comparison), then the use of different perceptions of institutional effectiveness can lead to erroneous and unfair conclusions (Hom, 2008). This is one pitfall that can make the peer group comparison risky. If the measurements of institutional effectiveness depend on different assumptions for institutional effectiveness, then the peer group analyst will probably stray into the swamp of comparing apples to oranges.

In terms of institutional research, the use of different perceptions of institutional effectiveness (and subsequently different definitions of it) in different studies can hinder the advancement of knowledge in institutional effectiveness. In particular, researchers who conduct research synthesis (that is, meta-analysis) can face a big problem. In these analyses, they use statistical methods to combine the results of different studies to estimate an overall effect size for some program element or intervention (Hunter and Schmidt, 1990). If the researcher finds that many of the studies on institutional effectiveness use different definitions of institutional effectiveness (based on different perceptions of it), then that researcher may be unable to conduct the meta-analysis on the remaining small number of studies that do share a common definition of institutional effectiveness. Aside from the practice of meta-analysis, the absence of standard methodology (consistency in definition for institutional effectiveness across studies) will impede the customary research goal of testing rival explanations for a specific phenomenon. Literature reviews in papers published in academic journals frequently include caveats about how prior studies have inconsistently defined a critical variable (which institutional effectiveness tends to be), making it necessary to conduct yet another study on a topic.

Situations also exist in which differing perceptions can help institutions. Divergent perceptions tend to highlight specific populations or specific needs that decision makers may overlook in the rush to act. In this respect, different perceptions of institutional effectiveness help to prevent the neglect of some stakeholders who may lack power or visibility. Divergent perceptions can reduce the risks of groupthink (Janis, 1982). The consideration of multiple views of institutional effectiveness can force decision makers to think more broadly about a situation, and this can possibly lead to a better decision than one relying on a single perception of institutional effectiveness. Finally, from a strategic planning perspective, divergent perceptions of institutional effectiveness can lead an institution to a new path for improvement if the divergent perceptions offer sound, innovative approaches to decision makers.

To some extent, divergent perceptions of institutional effectiveness can advance knowledge about institutional effectiveness as well. Researchers often try to see how robust a particular finding really is. That is, they seek to test the strength of a study result by comparing that one result to results of studies conducted under different assumptions (Cook and others, 1992). If such a comparison were to find strong agreement among all of the results despite differences in assumptions, then that one study's result would gain in terms of validity and credibility.

Despite instances where a lack of consensus helps advance research, the prevailing wisdom is that consensus plays a larger role than divergence. Pfeffer (2003) presents a strong argument about how the lack of consensus on models and methodology among researchers retards the advancement of knowledge in a discipline and limits the power that researchers in that field can attain. Although his immediate focus was the advancement of knowledge in the field of organizational behavior, he makes it clear how important a consensus can be for researchers in all disciplines—a principle that applies also to educational research and institutional research. He wrote, "An area of inquiry characterized by diffuse perspectives, none of which has the power to institutionalize its dominance, is one in which consensus is likely to remain elusive and the dispersion in resources, rewards, and activity will be great"(Pfeffer, 2003, p. 43). But Pfeffer qualifies this conclusion by warning about decreeing the use of one model or methodology when he says, "The question for organizational science is whether the field can strike an appropriate balance between theoretical tyranny and an anything-goes attitude" (p. 44).

NEW DIRECTIONS FOR COMMUNITY COLLEGES • DOI: 10.1002/cc

Responses

To take into account differing stakeholder perceptions and guard against some of the problems mentioned earlier, institutions should:

- Measure the differences or similarities in perceptions of institutional effectiveness that stakeholders may have (through focus groups or surveys, or both)
- Analyze the differences (perhaps with tools like the value tree)
- Where necessary, build consensus through tools like the Delphi method, cross-functional teams, and broadened frames of reference
- Use tools such as brainstorming in situations where the institution needs to rethink or broaden how it perceives and handles institutional effectiveness

The situation where college officials have little or no idea about the variation in perceptions on institutional effectiveness should warrant data collection (usually by surveys) so that officials can develop some idea of how divergent these perceptions really are among their relevant stakeholders. The absence of information about how different stakeholders view institutional effectiveness can have undesirable consequences. Stakeholders may believe that they share a perception when they actually disagree on one or more fundamental issues. In other situations, stakeholders may believe that their perceptions disagree when they actually agree. March (1994) concludes, "The former case leads to 'unwarranted' trust. The latter leads to 'unwarranted' distrust" (p. 112).

One way to inform decision makers would be a survey of stakeholders that leads to a value tree for each stakeholder (or stakeholder group if the researcher chooses to aggregate survey responses). If the survey results and value trees reveal a meaningful variation in perceptions, then the college should consider some sort of consensus-building process. If college officials decide that they want to build consensus, then they can consider the so-called Delphi method (Linstone and Turoff, 1975), which provides a systematic approach that can lead to consensus while limiting interpersonal friction in the process. In the first step in this process, a monitor or moderator polls a set of stakeholders for their ratings of a subject and tabulates the results. In the situation here, the monitor would ask stakeholders to offer a definition of institutional effectiveness. The monitor then sends this tabulation to the stakeholders, and each stakeholder gets an invitation to change his or her initial survey response. The monitor polls the stakeholders a second time in order to create a new tabulation that will integrate any changes that stakeholders may have made to their initial responses. Depending on time, cost, and topic difficulty, this process of tabulation, sharing, and adjustment may go through additional iterations. To reduce interpersonal conflict, the polling occurs such that each stakeholder can privately submit the rating; therefore, the stakeholders do not even need to be in the same room for the Delphi method to work.

Colleges could improve agreement among stakeholders on the issue of institutional effectiveness by other common organizational practices. Giving stakeholders roles in different committees or groups, using cross-functional or interdisciplinary teams, emphasizing institution-wide success, and publicizing the interdependence of the organization's subunits, for example, often enable stakeholders to expand their perception of institutional effectiveness to become an institution-wide view rather than a subunit view. Although movement away from a subunit perception toward an institution-wide perception will not necessarily lead to a consensus on what institution-wide effectiveness means, at least the breadth of the perception may become broad enough to create some convergence of perceptions.

Although I recommend the focus group approach for collecting data on divergent perceptions among stakeholders, I recommend against this approach as a consensus-building approach. As Morgan and Krueger (1993) unequivocally state, "Do not use focus groups when the primary intent is something other than research. . . . Unfortunately, there is a constituency that wants to apply the term *focus groups* to other purposes, such as resolving conflicts, building consensus, increasing communication, changing attitudes, and making decisions" (p. 11). In essence, the focus group method is not designed to attain these other purposes, and the misapplication of the method will probably lead to disappointing results.

It is also possible to benefit from diversity in perceptions about institutional effectiveness. In some situations, colleges may seek to generate different perceptions. A common tool for eliciting and generating such diverse perceptions is brainstorming. In general, institutional leaders can promote a diversification of perceptions by ensuring that stakeholders who voice a different perception can do so in an environment that is candid, rewarding, secure, and respectful.

Conclusion

The various stakeholders in the community college hold different perceptions of institutional effectiveness because the forces behind diversification in perception generally outweigh the forces behind consensus building in perception. However, a consensus may develop when a profound and tangible threat to this common interest arises. Two major threats that come immediately to mind are loss of accreditation and loss of public funding. Ironically, both threats may impose a single definition on the community college through the formal authority of off-campus parties. Whether the imposition of a single perception of institutional effectiveness is harmful or helpful to the long-term success of a community college could still benefit from an in-depth analysis.

In some respects, an imposed perception may integrate multiple perspectives so that the different perceptions of the different stakeholders can be leveraged rather than tolerated. California's state-run accountability system for community colleges takes such an approach (California Community Colleges Chancellor's Office, 2009). It considers a well-defined set of performance indicators in its annual review of institutional effectiveness, and these measures embrace the different interests connected to transfer, degree completion, career technical education, basic skills development, and English as a Second Language. Stakeholders may achieve some agreement on what counts as institutional effectiveness if that concept is inclusive enough to serve both their separate and common interests.

Finally, perceptions of institutional effectiveness grow enormously in importance when one compares how well an institution actually performs to how well stakeholders think it should perform. Even if all stakeholders can agree about what to measure and report in institutional effectiveness, a far greater challenge lies in deciding how well a college should perform. Expectations for the level of institutional performance, regardless of the set of performance indicators used, must reconcile diverse perceptions, and often competing ones, about how well a college should perform given community needs and the resources available. In a nutshell, knowing what a college has done will not tell decision makers what a college must do in the future. The institutional researcher can help address this greater challenge by providing analyses of performance in terms of inputs and outputs and by facilitating consensus building and stakeholder inclusion with tools like the Delphi method and the MAUT. But in the end, stakeholders will need to use value judgments, in addition to institutional research, in a political arena to shape perceptions and decisions about how well the community college must perform in the future.

References

California Community Colleges Chancellor's Office. *Focus on Results: Accountability Reporting for the California Community Colleges.* Sacramento: California Community Colleges Chancellor's Office, 2009. Retrieved Jan. 14, 2010, from http://www.cccco.edu/Portals/4/TRIS/research/ARCC/arcc_2009_final.pdf.
Cook, T., and others. *Meta-Analysis for Explanation.* New York: Russell Sage Foundation, 1992.
Edwards, W., and Newman, J. "Multiattribute Evaluation." In T. Connolly, H. Arkes, and K. Hammond (eds.), *Judgment and Decision Making.* Cambridge: Cambridge University Press, 2000.
Hom, W. "Peer Grouping: The Refinement of Performance Indicators." *Journal of Applied Research in the Community College,* 2008, 16(1), 45–51.
Hunter, J., and Schmidt, F. *Methods of Meta-Analysis.* Thousand Oaks, Calif.: Sage, 1990.
Janis, I. *Groupthink: Psychological Studies of Policy Decisions and Fiascos.* Boston: Houghton Mifflin, 1982.
Linstone, H., and Turoff, M. *The Delphi Method: Techniques and Applications.* Reading, Mass.: Addison-Wesley, 1975.

March, J. A. *Primer on Decision Making.* New York: Free Press, 1994.

Morgan, D., and Krueger, R. "When to Use Focus Groups and Why." In D. Morgan (ed.), *Successful Focus Groups: Advancing the State of the Art.* Thousand Oaks, Calif.: Sage, 1993.

Pfeffer, J. "Barriers to the Advancement of Organizational Science: Paradigm Development as a Dependent Variable." In L. Thompson (ed.), *The Social Psychology of Organizational Behavior.* New York: Psychology Press, 2003.

WILLARD C. HOM *is the director of research and planning in the technology, research, and information systems division of the Chancellor's Office, California Community Colleges, in Sacramento, California.*

9

Forces inside and outside community colleges are changing the context for performance and mandating new conceptions of effectiveness.

The Future of Institutional Effectiveness

Richard L. Alfred

Institutional effectiveness in the fast-paced market that community colleges have operated in for more than two decades is a product of unparalleled expansion. In this market, two basic constructs have served as a basis for measuring effectiveness: a numerator—growth and resources—and a denominator—outputs. Growth in the form of rising enrollments, incremental revenue, and anything else that can be counted is easily calculated and grasped. It is an attractive gauge of effectiveness for leaders looking for quick and easy evidence of success. Outputs—results generated with learners and stakeholders—are not as easily calculated nor are numbers measuring them easily understood. Ironically, while effectiveness models in colleges today focus primarily on outputs, leaders and staff working in a world of enrollments and resources focus on growth. What this suggests is that for leaders, the bigger return on investment may come from working with the numerator rather than measuring the denominator.

The implications of this contradiction for community colleges are many. Chief among them is a disjuncture in how leaders and staff may see effectiveness. Assessment specialists working in the microworld of methodology and numbers should ask themselves how well they understand the context in which effectiveness is measured. If their view of effectiveness includes only the denominator and they do not understand contextual forces influencing the numerator, their contribution to improving performance may be limited. The same is true for leaders working at the interface between institution and environment. If they do not pay attention to the denominator, their capacity to use results to leverage institutional perfor-

New Directions for Community Colleges, no. 153, Spring 2011 © 2011 Wiley Periodicals, Inc.
Published online in Wiley Online Library (wileyonlinelibrary.com) • DOI: 10.1002/cc.440

mance may be limited. Simultaneously attending to the numerator and denominator will be important for institutions that are serious about effectiveness.

This chapter addresses the future of institutional effectiveness in community colleges. Its emphasis is on what is measured and why, beginning with a retrospective look at early efforts in effectiveness, moving to an overview of models and methodologies in use today, and closing with a scenario for the future. The contribution of the past can be summed up with the observation that the issue of numerator and denominator has never been resolved. Effectiveness is a complex, multifaceted construct with a myriad of meanings and interpretations. It can be conceptualized and measured in the form of learner outcomes, institutional growth and change, value added, organizational efficiency, stakeholder satisfaction, ratings and rankings, and just about anything else that describes what institutions do. What colleges choose to measure and why is influenced by the context in which they operate. Accordingly, a significant portion of this chapter focuses on contextual conditions facing community colleges and their implications for effectiveness. The chapter closes with a discussion of effectiveness as paradox—an interpretation requiring colleges to simultaneously pursue contradictory approaches to effectiveness to get in front of the change curve.

Effectiveness: A Retrospective Look

Interest and attentiveness to effectiveness burgeoned in the early 1990s when community colleges entered a period of mission elaboration and enrollment growth. Part and parcel of growth were complexity and a belief that effectiveness was context and situation specific. No conception would prevail over time, nor would any model or measures be universally acceptable to all colleges (Alfred and Kreider, 1991).

The earliest effectiveness models focused on growth and reputation judged relative to other institutions (Roueche and Baker, 1987). As public calls for accountability escalated, new metaphors emerged with indicators of size and reputation no longer sufficient to demonstrate effectiveness. Community colleges were also expected to show evidence of value added through outcomes generated with learners. Different metaphors evolved over time, each adding to the criteria for effectiveness. For example, a metaphor that Alfred and Linder suggested in 1990 focused on the arena in which effectiveness was measured. Some aspects of performance were exclusively generated inside institutional walls (operational efficiency) and were labeled "inside-out," while others evolved outside the institution (employer satisfaction) and were labeled "outside-in." The California Association of Community Colleges developed a functional model of effectiveness in which indicators describing the performance of specific operating units or "functions" (educational programs, student services, academic support services, and so forth) served as a focal point for assessment

(Doucette and Hughes, 1990). Midlands Technical College in South Carolina developed and implemented a critical success factors approach to effectiveness in which assessment was focused on performance characteristics important to the success of the college and the expectations of its stakeholders (Hudgins, 1990).

These early approaches led to the development of the first edition of *Core Indicators of Effectiveness for Community Colleges* in 1994, a report written by a roundtable of community college educators representing different streams of work on effectiveness (Community College Roundtable, 1994). The goal of *Core Indicators* was to help community college practitioners respond coherently to a simple but important question: What are the key indicators of effectiveness in community colleges? The work of the roundtable focused primarily on student outcomes and stakeholder satisfaction as indexes of effectiveness and provided a working definition and technical descriptions for thirteen indicators. This volume was followed by a second edition of *Core Indicators* in 1999 that incorporated information about changing contextual conditions for effectiveness and expanded the number of indicators to fourteen by adding licensure and certification pass rates (Alfred, Ewell, Hudgins, and McClenney, 1999). New in this edition was cautionary advice regarding "red lights" that colleges needed to be aware of in effectiveness assessment and suggestions for responding to externally imposed measures. The third edition of *Core Indicators,* published in 2007, advanced the number of core indicators to sixteen by adding measures of student learning and general education competencies and presented a stage model that colleges with varying capability for assessment could use to measure effectiveness (Alfred, Shults, and Seybert, 2007).

The *Core Indicators* editions did much to advance our understanding of effectiveness, but they were limited by a linear conception of effectiveness. Their focus was exclusively on the denominator: outputs. They failed to account for the numerator—growth and resources—and contextual conditions shaping it. Moreover, they were written in the context of existing forces and conditions. The future was not the subject of speculation nor were ways of envisioning effectiveness based on intangibles such as stakeholder perceptions, faculty and staff satisfaction, and leveraging.

Change and Contradiction

Before the recession beginning in 2008, the future for community colleges was challenging but at least understandable. At the beginning of 2011, it is an uncharted horizon of simultaneously contradictory forces of growth and opportunity, resource decline, intensifying pressure for accountability, and changing rules of competition. Every college will encounter opportunities for growth and development that are part of a market loaded with customers wanting more and competitors offering more. Counterbalancing these opportunities, however, will be uncertainty about the resources that community colleges will have to support growth and their capacity to absorb growing legions of learners. These forces will have a significant impact on how colleges conceptualize and measure effectiveness.

Forces of Change.   Substantive change in the terrain for effectiveness can be traced back to 2008 with the onset of the recession and the election of Barack Obama as president. The recession profoundly disrupted every aspect of American life. Mobility ground to a sixty-year low as unemployment, plunging home values, and declining confidence in the economy forced people to delay major life decisions. The employment decline between October 2007 and April 2010 was the steepest on record since 1945 (U.S. Bureau of Labor Statistics, 2010). Millions of Americans became prisoners of their circumstances as the net worth of households dropped 22 percent from its peak in June 2007 (Federal Reserve Bank, 2010). A survey of 2,002 adults in April 2010 by Citi indicated that Americans, by more than a two-to-one margin, believed that they were worse off financially than they were the prior year (Clements, 2011). Some were unguardedly pessimistic about future prospects: for example, 36 percent of the adults surveyed believed the economy had hit bottom, but 59 percent believed economic conditions had not yet bottomed out. The mood of public officials paralleled the plight of citizens as governors in all but a few states indicated that state economies had hit bottom but were not yet in recovery, more federal government expenditures would be needed to create jobs and spur economic growth, and without renewal, exhausted stimulus funds would lead to further deterioration of public college and university operating budgets in fiscal years 2011 and 2012.

But in every cloud there is a silver lining. For community colleges, it has come in the form of rising visibility and dramatic enrollment growth. Enrollment increased by 10 to 20 percent between 2008 and 2009, and demand is expected to rise as community colleges become institutions of choice for displaced workers and families seeking relief from rising educational costs (Alfred, 2009). Growth, however, is not always positive. It has a downside realized in imbalance between demand and capacity when resources are insufficient to support growth. Colleges experiencing simultaneous forces of record enrollment growth and falling revenues have reached a breaking point in capacity. The instructional day has been extended, more part-time faculty have been hired, class size has been increased, and space has been acquired whenever and wherever possible. The large-scale addition of temporary staff has increased organizational size and complexity and further fragmented culture as new silos have emerged and existing silos have been reinforced. The dramatic increase in the rate of growth has prompted concerns about quality in institutions in which temporary staff deliver a significant portion of their core process.

With enrollment growth and problems with capacity have come policy initiatives that simultaneously favor community colleges and demand more of them. In 2009, the Obama administration launched a $12 billion completion initiative to boost the number of college graduates by 5 million by 2020. Community colleges will be on the receiving end of a sizable portion of this money, but strings are attached. They will be expected to value completion as much as access and to improve graduation rates significantly. This amounts to a dynamic of contradiction: community colleges will grow, but they will have less to work with and more will be expected of them.

The Dynamic of Contradiction.   Contrary forces of growth and decline could be likened to decelerators and accelerators. As decelerators, they constrain movement by constricting resources available to colleges, and as accelerators, they facilitate movement by encouraging change. Although community colleges are working with less, learners do not diminish their expectations and wait for them to catch up. They continually raise the bar on what they want and expect, and colleges must find ways to deliver or face consequences. In effect, decelerators become accelerators when leaders and staff must find creative solutions to adversity.

Accelerators and decelerators make up a dynamic of contradiction that will shape the context for effectiveness in the future. On the one hand, if forces of deceleration—a slowly recovering economy, declining public support, and diminished capacity—maintain their grip, enrollment could plateau as institutional capacity falls short of demand. If colleges choose to deliver more of their core process through temporary staff, nagging questions about quality and accountability could emerge. Stakeholders believing they are getting less will invariably push for more, with the result that leaders may be forced to divert resources from access to performance. Institutions focusing on growth and failing to attend to outputs will do so at their own peril in a policy landscape requiring incremental evidence of accountability.

If the economy instead moves through a sustained recovery, a scenario driven purely by forces of deceleration is unlikely. During a recovery, people return to a pattern of consumption, resulting in increased spending and an influx of revenue into state treasuries that eventually finds its way into community college operating budgets and fuels new growth. For community colleges, the implication of simultaneous conditions of growth and reduction would be one of paradox. While coping with the effects of deceleration fueled by lingering recession, they will simultaneously be coping with forces of acceleration fueled by calls for growth and accountability. Learners will want more and better service, and policymakers will push for evidence of better results. The implication for community colleges will be a future in which multiple approaches to the conception and measurement of effectiveness are employed to address contradictory conditions.

Paradox of the Future

Effectiveness is likely to operate in two realms in the future—one that can be called objective and the other subjective. These realms are contradictory

in nature and contribute to a condition of paradox that will mark the future
of effectiveness in community colleges.

Objective Realm.   The term *objective* refers to events in the realm of
experience that are independent of individual thought and readily percep-
tible to all observers. Indicators consensually recognized as fundamental to
the mission of community colleges, deeply embedded in external mandates,
and of high importance to important stakeholders can be said to comprise
an objective basis for effectiveness. Indeed, the indicators making up this
realm are integral to the effectiveness models in most colleges:

- Rate of growth (enrollment, programs, budgets, staff, facilities, and so
  forth)
- Efficiency (use of resources)
- Persistence
- Graduation rate
- Success in subsequent related course work
- Program learning outcomes and mastery of discipline
- General education competencies
- Career program placement rates
- Licensure and certification pass rates
- Client satisfaction with programs and services
- Transfer rate
- Performance after transfer

The basis for effectiveness models in the objective realm is the ability
of a college to produce outputs that correspond to statements of purpose in
its mission and vision (Ewell, 1992) and the needs and expectations of its
stakeholders (Alfred, 2005). This implies that the mission of a college and
the outcomes it generates are consistent with a growing variety of stakeholder needs. Nothing is more transparent to stakeholders than simply
reported numbers measuring the "objective" face of effectiveness—particularly measures related to end goals like degree completion, transfer, and job
attainment and advancement. Because the numbers that make up this realm
are central to what community colleges do and what is expected of them, it
is reasonable to expect that they will be part of the effectiveness equation in
the foreseeable future.

Subjective Realm.   We live in a world in which intangibles are
becoming increasingly important. Policymakers and practitioners alike
point to the growing importance of values, ideas, beliefs, and perceptions in
understanding performance in organizations. Whether a college performs
well or poorly is as much a function of stakeholder perceptions of the outcomes it generates as the outcomes themselves. In this way, effectiveness
has a subjective dimension realized in how audiences interpret the numbers generated in a college's objective realm.

The subjective realm of effectiveness, new to most colleges, will receive
increasing attention in the future. It will take at least three forms on most

campuses: valuation, in which effectiveness is a measure of the feelings people hold toward an institution; stretch, in which effectiveness is a measure of an institution's capacity to leverage its resources; and interpretation, in which effectiveness is a measure of a college's ability to create (and induce stakeholders to accept) new and different conceptions of success.

Effectiveness as Valuation. Valuation—the process through which stakeholders form perceptions of colleges by the results they generate and report—will become as important a contributor to effectiveness as the results themselves. Effectiveness is not absolute: it is linked to feelings and beliefs, and it is a product of the experience people have with institutions. Most of today's effectiveness models were created when linear relationships prevailed between institutions and stakeholders. Tomorrow's models will be sensitive to the fact that the influence of stakeholders has grown, and more information is needed from them to gauge a college's performance. Effectiveness will become a correlate of the relationship between stakeholder needs and satisfaction. Factors that change or alter this relationship will need to be identified and measured. For example, as competitors and technology change the rules of customer service, the connection between what stakeholders want (more and better service) and satisfaction (experience that meets or exceeds expectations) will need to be reexamined. Conventional indicators will have some utility in measuring this connection, but they may not dig deeply enough into the minds of individual stakeholders to uncover deeply seated feelings and beliefs.

We can illustrate the importance of valuation in effectiveness using a customer service analogy. If currently enrolled students indicate they are satisfied with college support services on routine surveys but still transfer or drop out what is really being measured? Conventional effectiveness models would leapfrog the process indicators involved in satisfaction and focus on outcomes—one of which would be nonpersistence. These models are not designed to measure student satisfaction as a function of the difference between what students want and expect and what they are getting. Future-focused effectiveness models will pay more attention to deeply embedded feelings students develop and hold toward the institution. In contrast to close-ended surveys that elicit surface impressions, these models will employ methods of data gathering that probe beneath the surface of what students are thinking and find out how they really feel. Factors typically not included in surveys, such as the nature and variety of contacts with faculty and staff, difficulty in accessing and using services, and feelings of social and cultural isolation, will be probed and their effect on satisfaction determined.

What valuation will bring to effectiveness in the future is the realization that community colleges will need to find new ways of measuring things that really count. They will learn not to rely solely on outcome measures and conventional techniques for gathering information. They will create breakthroughs in information depth and substance by incorporating measures of process into effectiveness models and using information-gathering techniques that uncover stakeholders' deepest concerns.

Effectiveness as Stretch.   When colleges rely primarily on indicators of output to measure effectiveness, attention goes to indexes that gauge the bottom line: the rate of growth, learner outcomes, placement rates, and the like. Institutions facing tough market conditions and diminishing resources experience a different reality that affects their approach to effectiveness. Intangibles underlying performance like organizational culture, employee satisfaction, and motivation have as much to do with outcomes. It will not be enough for leaders to run numbers related to growth and learner outcomes to establish that a college is doing well or poorly. They will also need to run numbers that gauge a college's ability to leverage its resources and, in so doing, enhance its capacity. This is called *stretch,* and it refers to an institution's capacity to achieve superior performance—that is, to maximize effectiveness—by optimizing its resources (Alfred, Shults, Jaquette, and Strickland, 2009).

How would stretch work in the effectiveness equation for community colleges? An obvious problem for colleges experiencing sustained erosion of resources will be locating new sources of revenue to support growth and maintain performance. By focusing explicitly on intangible resources such as people, ideas, culture, and tacit knowledge, stretch will encourage institutions and leaders to broaden their view of effectiveness to include often overlooked human dynamics that are important to performance (Alfred, Shults, Jaquette, and Strickland, 2009). Feldman and Khademian (2003) provide a good illustration in their examination of empowerment and cascading vitality in organizations resulting from the virtuous behavior of leaders. Actions that leaders take to empower staff work to improve relationships between individuals, organizations, and communities; increase engagement; and result in improved performance. Employee engagement leads to increased meaningfulness in work through its effect on job design, which in turn results in more motivated employees. In other words, positive actions or events at the individual level (empowerment by leaders) can lead to favorable outcomes at the organizational level (improved performance through employee engagement) that can create positive outcomes for the individual (meaningfulness).

Conceptualization and measurement of stretch could become an important dimension of effectiveness for community colleges because of its amplifying effect on resources. It does not develop without internal cohesion, so cohesion will become a goal within many colleges and efforts will be made to define and measure it. End measures (outcomes) will be seen as insufficient in and of themselves for assessing effectiveness. Effective colleges will be seen as those that emphasize, and are able to document, stretch in addition to outcomes.

NEW DIRECTIONS FOR COMMUNITY COLLEGES • DOI: 10.1002/cc

Effectiveness as Interpretation.   Since their inception, community colleges have been subjected to traditional definitions of completion and student success by external agencies. As a result, the focus of effectiveness models has narrowed over time to tested measures of outcomes, and creative thinking has atrophied. Now, however, community colleges are under significant pressure to focus on completion and to push more students across the finish line. The usual agents of accountability—government agencies, accrediting associations, and foundations—are clear about their expectations for completion and show no signs of backing off.

As institutions and leaders cope with increased pressure for completion, they will come to understand that it will not be enough to "do better" on traditional measures of success—to incrementally increase the number of graduates or completers. Instead they will need to establish new criteria for success by reinterpreting what completion means while simultaneously improving performance on established measures. To accomplish this, they will need to tap into the creative instincts of faculty and staff to frame new conceptions of "finished products," new completion structures, and new ways of measuring completion. They will begin this process by asking five questions of themselves:

- *What is the reality of completion for students enrolled in this institution?* In most institutions, a predictable pattern of results forms with entering student cohorts. Norms for completion are established as the proportion of learners graduating, transferring prior to graduation, dropping out, and so on remains constant from year to year. This pattern says a lot about an institution's potential for creating finished products. Strategically thinking leaders will use it to gauge the need within their institutions for new conceptions of completion.
- *Do we assign equal importance to completion and access?* Colleges that make meaningful inroads into student completion begin by underscoring its importance and assigning it equal value with access. They understand, however, that mandates do not guarantee commitment. They program in intangibles in the form of leaders and staff who can transform a belief in the importance of completion into the reality of achievement. Even the most compelling belief will lose its power if it floats unconnected above the everyday reality of organizational life. Identifying people and devising processes to bridge commitment to completion into the everyday work of staff is a role that leaders play in colleges with a capacity to innovate.
- *Are the hydraulics of our college—its mission, policies, culture, organizational architecture, systems and processes, and operations—designed to encourage high levels of completion?* Hydraulics are the mechanisms by which institutions translate mission, objectives, and resources into aligned action by individuals throughout the organization. In many colleges, attention to completion lags when the organization is overloaded

with multiple and conflicting priorities. Leaders interested in optimizing completion pay careful attention to the relationship between hydraulics and institutional goals and take purposeful steps to ensure convergence.

- *Do we have the imagination and creativity to envision new forms of completion and devise practical plans for implementation?* In colleges willing to experiment with new conceptions of completion, investment in ideas is as important as problem solving and operations. Leaders in these colleges encourage staff to engage in conversations that open the door to innovation. These conversations focus on questions that cut to the core of issues surrounding completion: What will "completion" mean in the future, and how will it differ from what it means today? What forms must completion take to meet the changing needs of students and external stakeholders? How do we need to change the institution to embrace new forms of completion? How can we commit people to new and different forms of completion?

- *Do we have the resources and wherewithal to convince external audiences to accept alternative conceptions of completion?* Colleges experimenting with completion will be lauded for their efforts, but effort will be inconsequential unless they are able to convince funding agencies and policymakers to accept new conceptions of completion. This will be a tough sell because of ingrained attitudes and policy implications, but it is essential if community colleges are to level the playing field for completion.

By forging new conceptions of completion and legitimizing them with external audiences, community colleges will essentially broaden the framework for effectiveness. New outcomes will be factored into effectiveness models including credentials, course packages leading to meaningful employment, life experience, and myriad curricular and cocurricular experiences that more fully and accurately depict what completion means in community colleges.

Conclusion

New applications of effectiveness will evolve as contextual conditions change and require community colleges to do more and better with less— more service for more learners and better outcomes with fewer resources. The arena for effectiveness will expand to include intangibles that have an impact on institutional performance. Prominent in this arena will be measures of capacity and leverage that gauge how effectively institutions use resources. Implicit in all of this will be an urgency for action. Community colleges will need to adjust effectiveness models in accord with changing contextual conditions and craft interpretations of performance that fit the reality of the landscape, their resources, and their capacity.

References

Alfred, R. L. *Managing the Big Picture in College and Universities: From Tactics to Strategy.* New York: Praeger, 2005.

Alfred, R. L. "Navigating Change with a Conventional Organization." New Jersey Association of Community College Presidents, speech, Nov. 19, 2009.

Alfred, R. L., Ewell, P., Hudgins, J., and McClenney, K. *Core Indicators of Effectiveness for Community Colleges.* (2nd ed.) Washington, D.C.: Community College Press, 1999.

Alfred, R. L., and Kreider, P. "Creating a Culture of Institutional Effectiveness." *Community College Journal,* Apr.–May 1991, pp. 34–39.

Alfred, R. L., and Linder, V. *Rhetoric to Reality: Effectiveness in Community Colleges.* Ann Arbor, Mich.: Community College Consortium, 1990.

Alfred, R. L., Shults, C., Jaquette, O., and Strickland, S. *Community Colleges on the Horizon: Challenge, Choice, or Abundance.* Lanham, Md.: Rowman and Littlefield, 2009.

Alfred, R. L., Shults, C., and Seybert, J. *Core Indicators of Effectiveness for Community Colleges.* (3rd ed.) Washington, D.C.: Community College Press, 2007.

Clements, J. "New Citi Survey: Americans Are Mired in Economic Winter Despite Signs of Spring." Retrieved from http://new.citi.com/2010/04/new-citi-survey-americans-are-mired-in-economic-winter-despite-signs-of-spring.shtml on February 20, 2011.

Community College Roundtable. *Community Colleges: Core Indicators of Effectiveness.* Washington, D.C.: American Association of Community Colleges, 1994.

Doucette, D., and Hughes, B. (eds.). *Assessing Institutional Effectiveness in Community Colleges.* Laguna Hills, Calif.: League of Innovation, 1990.

Ewell, P. T. Outcomes Assessment, Institutional Effectiveness, and Accreditation: A Conceptual Exploration. Resource Paper for the Council on Postsecondary Accreditation Task Force on Institutional Effectiveness, 1992.

Federal Reserve Bank. *Q4 Flow of Funds Report.* Washington, D.C.: Federal Reserve Bank, Mar. 11, 2010.

Feldman, M. S., and Khademian, A. "Empowerment and Cascading Vitality." In K. S. Cameron, J. E. Dutton, and R. E. Quinn (Eds.), *Positive Organizational Scholarship: Foundations of a New Discipline.* San Francisco: Berrett-Koehler.

Hudgins, J. *Institutional Effectiveness Report Card.* Columbia, S.C.: Midlands Technical College, 1990.

Roueche, J., and Baker, G. *Access and Excellence: The Open-Door College.* Washington, D.C.: Community College Press, 1987.

U.S. Bureau of Labor Statistics. "Payroll Employment in 2009: Job Losses Continue." *Monthly Labor Review.* Washington, D.C.: Department of Labor, 2010.

RICHARD L. ALFRED *is professor of higher education at the University of Michigan and founding director of the Center for Community College Development.*

NEW DIRECTIONS FOR COMMUNITY COLLEGES • DOI: 10.1002/cc

INDEX

NEW DIRECTIONS FOR COMMUNITY COLLEGE

ORDER FORM SUBSCRIPTION AND SINGLE ISSUES

DISCOUNTED BACK ISSUES:

Use this form to receive 20% off all back issues of *New Directions for Community College*.
All single issues priced at **$23.20** (normally $29.00)

TITLE	ISSUE NO.	ISBN

*Call 888-378-2537 or see mailing instructions below. When calling, mention the promotional code JBNND
to receive your discount. For a complete list of issues, please visit www.josseybass.com/go/ndcc*

SUBSCRIPTIONS: (1 YEAR, 4 ISSUES)

☐ New Order ☐ Renewal

U.S.	☐ Individual: $89	☐ Institutional: $259
CANADA/MEXICO	☐ Individual: $89	☐ Institutional: $299
ALL OTHERS	☐ Individual: $113	☐ Institutional: $333

*Call 888-378-2537 or see mailing and pricing instructions below.
Online subscriptions are available at www.onlinelibrary.wiley.com*

ORDER TOTALS:

Issue / Subscription Amount: $ _____

Shipping Amount: $ _____
(for single issues only – subscription prices include shipping)

Total Amount: $ _____

SHIPPING CHARGES:

First Item	$5.00
Each Add'l Item	$3.00

*(No sales tax for U.S. subscriptions. Canadian residents, add GST for subscription orders. Individual rate subscriptions must
be paid by personal check or credit card. Individual rate subscriptions may not be resold as library copies.)*

BILLING & SHIPPING INFORMATION:

☐ **PAYMENT ENCLOSED:** *(U.S. check or money order only. All payments must be in U.S. dollars.)*

☐ **CREDIT CARD:** ☐ VISA ☐ MC ☐ AMEX

Card number _____ Exp. Date_____

Card Holder Name_____ Card Issue # _____

Signature _____ Day Phone_____

☐ **BILL ME:** *(U.S. institutional orders only. Purchase order required.)*

Purchase order # _____
Federal Tax ID 13559302 • GST 89102-8052

Name_____

Address_____

Phone_____ E-mail_____

Copy or detach page and send to: **John Wiley & Sons, PTSC, 5th Floor
989 Market Street, San Francisco, CA 94103-1741**

Order Form can also be faxed to: **888-481-2665**

PROMO JBNND